D1449034

Leading with Love

Leading with Love

…and Getting More Results

Neil Eskelin

Revell
A DIVISION OF
Baker Book House Co

© 2001 by Neil Eskelin

Published by Fleming H. Revell
a division of Baker Book House Company
P.O. Box 6287, Grand Rapids, MI 49516-6287

Printed in the United States of America

All rights reserved. No part of this publication may be reproduced, stored in a retrieval system, or transmitted in any form or by any means—for example, electronic, photocopy, recording—without the prior written permission of the publisher. The only exception is brief quotations in printed reviews.

Library of Congress Cataloging-in-Publication Data

Eskelin, Neil.
    Leading with love : and getting more results / Neil Eskelin.
       p. cm.
    Includes bibliographical references.
    ISBN 0-8007-5742-4
    1. Leadership. 2. Leadership—Religious aspects—Christianity. I.
Title.

    BF637.L4 E75 2001
    158´.4—dc21   2001034954

Unless otherwise noted, all Scripture is from the HOLY BIBLE, NEW INTERNATIONAL VERSION®. NIV®. Copyright © 1973, 1978, 1984 by International Bible Society. Used by permission of Zondervan Publishing House. All rights reserved.

Scripture marked KJV is taken from the King James Version of the Bible.

Scripture marked TLB is taken from *The Living Bible* © 1971. Used by permission of Tyndale House Publishers, Inc., Wheaton, IL 60189. All rights reserved.

Scripture marked NKJV is taken from the New King James Version. Copyright © 1979, 1980, 1982 by Thomas Nelson, Inc. Used by permission. All rights reserved.

For current information about all releases from Baker Book House, visit our web site:
http://www.bakerbooks.com

Contents

Introduction

For many, reading this book will be an uncomfortable experience. Reflecting on the stories, anecdotes, and examples, they will ask:

"Is this how people actually see me?"
"Does my personality really communicate these traits?"
"Is this my leadership style?"

Without knowing how it happened, countless well-intentioned people have adopted behavior patterns that others view as rude, arrogant, or brash. Often they will defend their actions, saying, "I just want to get results!"

On these pages you will discover that by leading with love—rather than through intimidation—you will achieve even *greater* results.

When love rules, the benefits are surprising.

Once, the famous pianist Paderewski was about to perform at a great concert hall. In the well-dressed, high-society audience a woman sat with her squirmy eight-year-old son. She hoped that by hearing this great artist, the boy would show more interest in his piano lessons.

Tired of waiting, the young man fidgeted in his seat. Then, as his mother talked with friends, he couldn't keep still any longer. The boy was drawn to the big black piano in the spotlight on stage. At first nobody seemed to notice him as he walked up the platform steps and sat down at the piano. Looking down at the keys he suddenly began to play "Chopsticks."

The now-hushed audience couldn't believe it! "Usher, stop that boy!" an outraged onlooker shouted. "Get him away from there!"

Paderewski heard the sounds on stage and quickly surmised what was happening. He rushed to the platform and, without uttering a word, stooped over the boy, reached around with both hands and began to play a counter-melody to "Chopsticks."

As they played the song together, the famed pianist kept whispering to the boy, "Don't stop, son. Keep playing!"

What a prelude to a concert! The audience loved more than the music—they loved Paderewski.

Every day we are given unexpected opportunities to touch lives. How we respond makes an indelible impression on others—plus it shapes our character and reputation. Some may say, "I'm too set in my ways to change." But as you will learn, when you combine a commitment of the heart with learned skills, the change is not only possible, it is *probable*.

Something else you will discover is that love-based leadership is not a sign of weakness; it communicates surprising strength.

I recall attending a committee meeting that was extremely tense. The president of the organization called several department heads together and said, "I'm about to make a recommendation to the board, and I want your input before I do."

There were nine people in the room, and each was given a chance to voice their opinion. Everyone endorsed the proposal until the ninth man stood to speak. He said, "I think this is the worst decision this institution could possibly make! I'm totally against it!"

The president asked for a vote. It was eight to one in favor of the recommendation. Instantly, the man who had dissented stood to his feet and announced, "I've told you how I feel. Now I want you to know something else. I believe in the democratic process and I believe in each of you. From this moment forward, you will never hear me say one negative word about this decision, and I am pledging my full support." And that's exactly what he did.

Leadership based on love is accompanied by loyalty. As the apostle Paul wrote to his friends at Corinth, "If you love someone you will be loyal . . . no matter what the cost" (1 Cor. 13:7 TLB).

On these pages we will answer the questions:

- What is the secret of motivating people?
- Why do authoritarian methods eventually fail?
- Is it possible to be both a servant and a king?
- What are the surefire methods of team building?
- How does love-based leadership work in a crisis?
- What are the keys to building shatterproof relationships?
- What are the specific qualities of leaders who love?

My desire is that the message of this book will capture your heart and transform your future. Remember, love is like the five loaves and two fishes. It does not begin to multiply until you give it away.

1

"The Flogging Will Stop When the Morale Improves!"

■ A revolution in leadership is happening at all levels of society—in schools, in business, in government, and even in our homes and churches. The era of autocratic, dictatorial authority is either dead or dying, and those who cling to "command and control" tactics are being both ridiculed and ignored.

Replacing these austere, judgmental, turf-building taskmasters is a surprising new breed of leaders. Their power comes from embracing diversity, encouraging innovation, sharing authority, and empowering those they serve.

"What's happening?" a high school administrator recently asked me. "For years I've worked for school superintendents who were absolute jerks. Now I have a boss whom I can only describe as being open, honest, sensitive, and caring."

What today's power players are discovering is not something new. They are recognizing long-neglected principles proclaimed centuries ago by men including Moses, Solomon, and Christ. Whether you are presiding over a Fortune 500 company, building a sales force, coaching a softball team, or simply trying to raise positive kids, the message of this book is essential.

Arrogant Authority

It's unfortunate, but some people just don't get it! The moment they rise to the position of "boss," a negative personality upheaval takes place. Far too often I've seen decent, mild-mannered individuals suddenly become aloof, arrogant, and ruthless when they are handed the reins of authority. Their motivational techniques sink to the level of the merchant ship captain who shouted: "The flogging will stop when the morale improves!"

Here's a sample of what people say who are demoralized in such an atmosphere:

"Incentives? That's hogwash. Threats and intimidation are all we ever see."

"She can't really have a heart! I've seen her trample over too many people to reach her goal."

"If you're going to get a promotion around here, you have to be a little callous—even if that means turning your back on a friend."

"To really succeed, you can't always be honest."

"I've got to look out for me! Others can take care of themselves!"

"I believe my boss would fire his own mother the night before Christmas!"

Many people still pay homage to the old Prussian military chain of command: Decisions are made at the top, transmitted through the middle, and executed at the bottom. Far too often, however, the execution comes from above.

"I thought that's how I was supposed to act," said the manager of a fast food restaurant in Phoenix who had just been fired for berating and intimidating his employees. It was the young man's first experience at being at the helm, and he was simply duplicating the only leadership model he had seen in action.

The time has long passed since those under supervision had no alternatives for their future. If they clash with the leadership style, there are thousands of "help wanted" notices awaiting their reply. It's not like Chicago's Cook County Jail, where a sign in the cafeteria reads: "This is not Burger King! We do not do it your way. This is the county jail. We will do it our way!"

If you think back for a moment about each of the personalities to whom you have been accountable, there is certain to be one boss who stands alone as "most negative." A Texas high school football player made this observation of his coach: "At least he's fair. He treats us all the same—like dogs!"

In effect, many leaders talk from both sides of their mouth. They attempt to sugarcoat their directives, yet hidden behind their words are grenades and rocket launchers waiting to explode on those who fail to obey. Many handle their subordinates as Al Capone did. He once stated, "You can get more with a kind word and a gun than you can get with a kind word."[1]

It is distressing when you cross paths with a superior who treats his or her charges much like the soldiers of the Light Brigade that Alfred Lord Tennyson wrote about:

> Theirs not to make reply,
> Theirs not to reason why,
> Theirs but to do and die.

When you examine the leadership of some companies, you come to the conclusion that tough-skinned dinosaurs still exist. You can find old-style chiefs who are rigid, demanding, formal, and paternalistic. And, if you close your eyes, you can almost hear Archie Bunker saying, "When I want your opinion, Edith, I'll give it to you!"

Theory X and Y

Douglass McGregor, professor of business at the Massachusetts Institute of Technology, articulated two distinct theories of why employees behave in certain ways. He called them "Theory X" and "Theory Y."

Theory X: The average person has a basic dislike for work—they must be pushed and prodded into it. The only things they respond to are the threat of punishment, being fired, or to financial incentives. They would much rather be directed by someone else than to accept responsibility for themselves. As a result, workers need close supervision and can't be trusted to produce without continual oversight and direction.

Theory Y: Both mental and physical work is as natural for man as play or rest. Employees will commit themselves to tasks that satisfy their needs for self-respect and personal fulfillment. They will readily accept responsibility for meaningful work, especially if they are involved in its design; and they will provide their own self-discipline in striving to reach their goals.

It is vital that you take a moment to reflect on these two positions and determine which theory is at the core of your personal belief system. If you sincerely hold to the Theory X position, this volume will steer you toward a bold new adventure. However, if you are already in the Theory Y camp, the words on these pages will not only confirm your convictions but allow you to take a mega-leap forward.

The Power Shift

In earlier times, tactics of tyrants may have worked. Not today. Because of reasons we'll discuss, power has shifted from the corporate executive to the consumer, from the politician to the voter, from the teacher to the student, and from the preacher to those in the pew.

The revolution has spawned several new modes of leadership, yet there's only one that ultimately succeeds—the style that is the focus of this book.

Somehow we have come to the mistaken conclusion that a leader has to manipulate, direct, or control. Ultimate triumph, however, is not the result of demonstrating your power. Rather, it is found in discovering the virtue of empowering others.

Ask any great symphony director and they will tell you that technical musicianship is only part of the matrix in producing a great performance. Carlos Maria Giulini, conductor of the Los Angeles Philharmonic, claims that "what matters most of music making requires real friendship among those who work together."[2] When does the most beautiful music occur? When the musicians demonstrate true love and affection for the talented people who surround them.

We need to be constantly reminded of the words of the apostle Paul: "Each of you should look not only to your own interests, but also to the interests of others" (Phil. 2:4).

Five Dangers

Perhaps you believe there is no alternative for an autocratic style when embarking on a new enterprise or controlling a complex operation. Oh, it certainly takes a firm hand to guide the unwieldy growth of certain organizations, but dictatorial methods won't work in the long run for five reasons:

1. **The sharpest people always head for the door.**
   Those who are enough on the ball to land a new job or serve in a new cause leave the dictator to his own devices.
2. **The insecure, ineffective workers stay behind.**
   Eventually the organization has zero leadership—except for the autocrat.
3. **There is constant stress on the employees or volunteers.**
   Domineering decision making produces an atmosphere of anxiety and tension that even visitors can recognize.
4. **A dictator cannot afford to have one failure.**

Just one bad decision and the troops will pounce on the dictator's leadership and attempt to tear it apart.

5. **The quality of goods and services decreases because of a demoralized workforce.** The internal strife produced by oppressive leadership will eventually cause the bottom line or organizational mission to suffer greatly.

Command-and-control tactics may still find a home with basic military recruits; society, however, has been enlightened to the point that the vast majority of people will no longer tolerate domination. As William T. Solomon, chairman and CEO of Austin Industries, states, "There has been a massive change in corporate leadership in the last 20 years. Leadership and a sense of accountability for what really goes on in the organizations have been pushed down and distributed throughout the organization."[3]

Dictatorial methods may have sufficed in steel mills and manufacturing operations in past decades, but the world has radically changed. Today's generation is more concerned with people than with products.

It's no secret that top executives in both corporate and nonprofit organizations are under intense scrutiny—from boards who pay their often-inflated salaries, from workers who expect to be recognized and rewarded for their efforts, and from the users of the goods and services who demand attention and respect.

In this consumer-oriented age, the balance of power has truly shifted. It no longer flows from the top down but from the bottom up. It's a high-stakes game where the consumer is suddenly holding the most valued cards.

Who Is a Leader?

The dilemma facing most people in positions of author-ity is this: "How can I be both a tough, bottom-line man-ager and a caring, encouraging leader?"

An employee at a charitable foundation in Philadelphia found an appropriate name for his boss, calling him "a compassionate tyrant."

There is usually no correlation between leadership and the title on a person's business card. Just because some-one is called president, director, or CEO does not make that individual an effective captain. There are great lead-ers, those who are average, and those who are hardly wor-thy of the name—in spite of their impressive title.

The question may be asked: "Who is a leader?" Any-one—at any level—whose actions produce positive move-ment and direction. If you are such a person, you don't need to wait for a spacious corner office to exercise your abilities. You can now, right where you are.

You may also ask, "What is the difference between lead-ership and management?"

While leaders provide vision and direction, managers are commissioned to produce order and conformity. In other words, the manager makes the leader's vision operational.

In terms of history, our use of the word *management* is relatively new. The need arrived with the rise of the rail-roads and giant steel and textile mills of the past century. Thousands of people were hired to supervise the work forces of these colossal enterprises. Unfortunately, many organizations became over-managed and under-led. Yet out of the ranks of both workers and managers arose those with enormous leadership abilities. They not only raised some of these ventures to new heights but charted new paths of opportunity.

Are those same doors still open? Absolutely—and especially for those who embrace concern and compassion.

How can a person be transformed from haughty to humble, from tyrant to tender, and from slave-driver to servant? It begins with *you*. Tracy Goss, cofounder of the Leadership Center for Re-Invention, states, "If you are going to re-invent your organization, then in order to succeed, you must *first* re-invent yourself."[4]

Barriers to Change

If caring, concerned leadership is the wave of the future, why are so many drowning in the waters of the past?

- Do they have the wrong role model?
- Are they fearful of attempting a new method or style?
- Do they really believe fear and intimidation produce lasting results?
- Is their brusque attitude simply a mask for their lack of confidence?
- Are they incapable of expressing appreciation and affection?

These are just a few of the questions we will address as we detail what it means to be a leader who loves.

2

The Carrots and Sticks of Leadership

■ Recently, after I signed the papers to purchase a new car, the salesman confided to me, "Mr. Eskelin, you are going to receive a phone call from our company asking you a few questions about how you were treated."

"No problem," I chuckled. "I'll just tell them you haggled with me over the price until I almost walked out of the showroom." He knew those were not my sentiments, because I had never been treated with more courtesy and respect on a dealership floor.

"Don't even joke about it," he replied. "You have no idea how important your response during that phone survey is to me. If I did an excellent job, please tell them."

I learned that both team members and the entire dealership was rated by this Customer Satisfaction Index. Every associate was consumed with demonstrating care and attention from the moment a customer walked onto the premises.

Grocery Shopping

How do you persuade a rabbit to move forward? Do you beat him with a stick from behind, or dangle a carrot in front of his nose? In the short run, both tactics are effective—the rabbit will jump. If you want a happy hare, however, you'd better run to the produce department and stock up on carrots.

Far too many leaders are ineffective motivators because they have a warped idea of their role. Their inward thoughts are:

"They put me in charge, so I guess I'm supposed to have all the answers."

"If I'm the leader, I'm not allowed to make any mistakes."

"If you want things done right, you have to do it yourself."

"If we implement anything new around here, it should be my idea."

"In my position, no one should question my authority."

What are the results of such thinking? Workers with no will, a staff with no spirit, and followers with no fire.

I'm sure you have met executives who come from the Lion Tamer school of management: "Keep them well-fed and never let them know that all you've got is a chair and a whip." Instead we need to heed the example of John F. Welch Jr., chairman of General Electric. He declared, "We're going to win on our ideas, not by whips and chains."[1]

What's Your Style?

Like combining the colors of the rainbow, there are countless leadership styles. In most instances they fall into these five basic categories:

1. **Authoritarian**—A harsh, demanding, inflexible approach. "It's my way or the highway."
2. **Humanistic**—Doesn't follow a precise plan. Allows others to set the agenda. "What do you think we ought to do today?"
3. **Charismatic**—Depends upon personality for success. "Wow! I'm really excited about this!"
4. **Democratic**—Always seeking a consensus prior to moving ahead. "Before we go any further, let's take a vote."
5. **Mission-driven**—Builds a team to fulfill the organization's vision and purpose. "We're all in this thing together."

In the first four categories, the style is almost always a reflection of the person who is currently at the helm. When a leader is mission-driven, however, several important factors begin to emerge—most notably that the entire organization is pulling in the same direction. That means there is far less need for nudging the troops.

What Motivates?

While I was having dinner with a group of seasoned sales managers in Phoenix, the topic wound its way to "what makes people tick?" One gray-haired man spoke up with a phrase that at first didn't make sense. He said, "What motivates people is what motivates people."

I asked, "What do you mean?"

"It's simple," he replied. "Before you ever attempt to motivate someone you'd better take the time to find out what turns them on." In other words, it's not *your* motivation, but *theirs.*

He explained, "What good is it to announce a sales contest with the winner receiving a paid vacation to Costa Rica if everyone would rather go to Hawaii—or perhaps have the option of a cash bonus?"

Do your homework. Discover what people truly desire, and create a "carrot" linked to their dream.

The Rod and the Staff

How can you erase the image that you are carrying a baseball bat and pressuring people to perform? One proven method is to squash the symbols of power so that all of your associates feel they are on an equal footing. Here's how some have accomplished that objective:

- A bank manager in Norfolk removed his name from the most coveted parking spot and replaced it with a sign that read, "Employee of the Month." He parked with the rest of the staff.
- The guidance counselor at a middle school in Jacksonville decided to walk the halls and playgrounds two hours every day, engaging students in informal conversations.
- The head honcho of a computer software company in Palo Alto, California, halted the practice of eating lunch with his top people in the private executive

dining room. Instead he ate in the company cafeteria—making certain he sat at a different table each time.

- In Cleveland, the president of a wholesale paper company turned his office into an employee lounge and created a rather open office space for himself right in the middle of the warehouse.

Real life is not the military. You don't need a decorated uniform or colorful bars pinned to your shirt to indicate your rank. The position of a true captain is always recognized. Educator Lester Bittel observes, "Leadership that is wholly dependent on the authority of position or status is coercion rather than leadership."[2]

Grabbing the Hose!

Bob Teague, executive of a large heating and cooling corporation in North Carolina, told me about an obnoxious salesman who made a presentation in his office. "The man was attempting to sell us an employee training program for our employees and was bragging about the techniques he would use to motivate our staff," he recalled.

It didn't take Bob long to determine that if this fellow addressed his staff the sessions would be a disaster. In the middle of his sales pitch, the man paused and asked, "Mr. Teague, what motivational techniques have you used that were effective?"

Bob reached down into the bottom drawer of his desk and pulled out a twelve-inch piece of rubber hose. Shaking the hose in the air, he said, "If anybody gets out of line around here, I just bring them to my office and use this!"

He laughed as he told me how that salesman grabbed his catalog case and literally backed out of the door. Of course, Bob doesn't lead by intimidation. He really enjoyed telling me the story.

Push or Pull?

Isn't it strange that in a nation founded on freedom and liberty those values are often stifled at all levels of society? Certainly there should be guidelines, procedures, and codes of conduct, yet people need to be free of the restrictions that bind their creativity and talent.

Answer this question: Do you inspire people by pushing or by pulling?

Remember watching the dog acts at the circus? Every time they jumped through a hoop or did a flip, their master would reward them with something to eat. Those creatures didn't learn their tricks through punishment but with prizes.

You don't need to slam a two-by-four over the head of a mule to get his attention. Simply place a bowl of oats in the direction you want him to move. I am convinced that when the right vision is placed before an individual, they will be drawn to it like steel is attracted to a magnet.

Rewards, premiums, and bonuses work. And they will be far more effective when the prize is for accomplishing an objective created by the worker, not by you. How is that possible? Simply allow people to have input into the project and let them take ownership of the process.

I remember attending a board meeting where the chairman gave a highly opinionated presentation promoting a controversial project. Then he said, "Now I'd like to have your comments."

After hearing a statement from each member on the board, the chairman restated the member's observation to fit his pre-ordained plan. It didn't take long for members to realize their input was being distorted by a chief who was twisting their personal opinions. When the vote on the project was finally taken, it was nine to one—against!

Instead of winning converts with persuasion and logic, he attempted to force the board into a decision. John Kotter, professor of organizational behavior at Harvard Business School, makes this observation: "Controls are purely driven by the head, whereas inspiration often comes from the heart. The one focuses on surface behavior and its effects, the other on the deepest reaches of the human soul."[3]

Touching Lives

Why does motivation wrapped in love succeed? It works because you are using a person-to-person approach. Change does not happen because of an elaborate scheme or a detailed program. It takes place because one individual makes an impact on the life of another.

According to author John Katzenbach, a guiding force in the movement for organizational change, innovative leaders—while in very short supply in most large organizations—are surprisingly easy to identify. "You simply ask executives for the names of people with a reputation for improving performance through people—and for exceeding expectations along the way."[4] What is the key? People.

To move any organization ahead, whether it be a computer company, a youth group, or a family, you can't treat people as faceless numbers or "units." True resources involve much more than inventory or finances. David Pincus, a specialist in management and employee communications, observes, "Old-line CEOs believed in the bottom line, first, last, and always. New-line CEOs appreciate the bottom line too, but they also recognize the hidden value of human resources."[5]

Pour on the Praise

Recently I received a letter from a man residing in Chicago who attended a "Leaders Are Lovers" seminar. As I read his comments I remembered him approaching me after the session, saying, "I've tried balancing discipline and love with my fifteen-year-old son and it doesn't seem to work."

"Well, tell me about your ratio?" I asked. "How much discipline and how much love?"

He thought for a second and concluded, "Oh, I'd say it's fifty–fifty."

"Whoa!" I exclaimed. "That's far too much discipline. Why don't you try 90 percent affection and 10 percent correction?"

He wrote in his letter, "Neil, the 90 percent love potion has worked wonders. It's been years since I've had this kind of relationship with my son."

The successful cosmetics entrepreneur Mary Kay Ash advises people to "sandwich every bit of criticism between two heavy layers of praise."[6] That's a great place to start. Now keep pouring on the praise.

REMINDERS FOR LEADERS WHO LOVE

- Chart and measure your care and attention.

- Destroy your whips and chains.
- Adopt a mission-driven leadership style.
- Don't invent motivation—tap into people's desires.
- Greatly decrease the symbols of power.
- Offer rewards and premiums, not rebukes and punishment.
- Never twist opinions to fit your agenda.
- Increase your praise-to-discipline ratio.
- Love people, not programs.

Those who have been placed in your care aren't rabbits, yet perhaps you would be wise to treat them as such. It's time to build a bonfire with your canes and hickory sticks. Start preparing a banquet that will have your associates shouting "More!"

3

What Sheep Expect from Shepherds

■ While driving through Israel I came across a scene that could have been painted thousands of years earlier. We pulled to the side of the road to watch a solitary shepherd who was faithfully keeping watch over his flock of several hundred sheep.

He was crouched down, holding a staff in his hand—rarely allowing his eyes to wander.

The sheep, foraging for nourishment, didn't seem to notice their master. You can rest assured, however, they knew his exact location and the reason for his presence. The dynamic at work on that parched pasture was twofold: Both the leader and the followers believed their counterpart would behave in certain, predictable ways.

Ten Expectations

As a parent, teacher, or executive, you have also been given an assignment that carries a heavy responsibility. And while it is true that many decisions are allowed to be made at lower levels on the chain of command, people continue to look to the top for both direction and protection. Specifically, individuals desire that you will fulfill these ten expectations:

1. Sheep expect shepherds to be concerned for their safety. When people are asked to rank the values or attributes they most admire in a leader, "providing job security" is high on the list. They want the assurance that their organization is healthy, wealthy, and wise—wise enough to survive in turbulent times and provide for their future.

Workers aren't dense. They are fully aware that in these changing economic times their workplace could be sold, merged, or perhaps something far worse. The supervisor of an audio components manufacturing plant in Missouri said, "Listening to the rumors flying around here makes my stomach churn. I expect that any day they'll tell us our jobs have been moved to Mexico or Thailand. There's no one denying anything, or giving us reassurance."

Everybody wants to know the weather report, yet some leaders hide the fact there are ominous clouds and insecurity looming on the horizon. A protector who is concerned with the welfare of his flock won't hesitate to communicate both the possibilities and the perils. A great leader will take extraordinary measures to safeguard the future of his employees.

2. Sheep expect shepherds to find green pastures. I talked with a rancher in New Mexico who told me, "One great difference between sheep and cattle is that sheep will chew the grass so close to the soil there is hardly anything left."

Can you imagine the ultimate fate of a flock that was never guided or allowed to move forward? They'd die from lack of food.

Whether you are operating a restaurant, retreat center, or a real estate agency, if you're stagnant you won't survive. What kind of leadership is necessary? It is the dynamic, active type written about by the psalmist.

> The LORD is my shepherd; I shall not want. He maketh me to lie down in green pastures: he leadeth me beside the still waters.
>
> Psalm 23:1–2 KJV

3. Sheep expect shepherds to know them by name. How close is your link to those you serve? Close enough that you can call each of them by their first name?

One of the great parables given by Jesus contrasted the difference between a "good shepherd" and one who did not properly care for his sheep. He explained that when a responsible shepherd enters the gate, "the sheep listen to his voice. He calls his own sheep by name and leads them out. When he has brought out all his own, he goes on ahead of them, and his sheep follow him because they know his voice" (John 10:3–4). Then he added, "But they will never follow a stranger; in fact they will run away from him because they do not recognize a stranger's voice" (v. 5).

We simply cannot underestimate the value of establishing an individual connection with every person on our team—even if that number is large. The bond is strengthened each time they hear you speak their name.

4. Sheep expect shepherds to be gentle and kind. Recently I heard the head of a nonprofit organization complain about the grief and aggravation he had been receiving from those on his staff. "Sheep bite," he stated.

When people you serve are less than cooperative, it's not an excuse for retaliation. As Dwight Eisenhower said about his experiences in World War II, "You do not lead by hitting people over the head—that's assault, not leadership."[1]

A nurse at a retirement home once confided, "I can't begin to tell you the stress I am under. I'm sure my supervisor would treat any dog or cat with more humanity than we experience around here."

If you feel the urge to become demanding and difficult, instead of lashing out at those around you, get tough on yourself. That's where discipline always yields the greatest harvest.

Listen to the words of Isaiah:

> He tends his flock like a shepherd:
>   He gathers the lambs in his arms
> and carries them close to his heart.
>
> Isaiah 40:11

5. *Sheep expect shepherds to rescue them when they stray.* Centuries ago, the Roman playwright Publius Syrus observed this basic fact about human nature: "We are interested in others when they are interested in us."

What is your response when a member of your family, or one of your employees, becomes distracted and sidetracked? Do you let them stay off course and struggle to find their own way back, or do you stop what you're doing and give them your total attention?

Remember these words spoken by Christ. "Suppose one of you has a hundred sheep and loses one of them. Does he not leave the ninety-nine in the open country and go after the lost sheep until he finds it?" (Luke 15:4).

Ted Briggs, the manager of a chemical lawn care service in Atlanta, says, "I can't stand the thought of losing one customer. If they don't renew, I stop by their home personally to learn the reason why."

6. *Sheep expect shepherds to be fearless.* You must be awake and alert to danger—and when your organization is under immediate threat, it's time for daring and courage.

As a child I always enjoyed the dramatic story of little David, with five stones and a slingshot, coming against mighty Goliath. Later, I read the words the young man said to King Saul before he faced the giant. "Your servant has been keeping his father's sheep. When a lion or a bear came and carried off a sheep from the flock, I went after it, struck it and rescued the sheep from its mouth" (1 Sam. 17:34–35).

It took guts for David to challenge the legend of the Philistines, yet because he had some experience, it bolstered his self-confidence.

If you have won a victory, however small, use it as a stepping stone to enter the larger battlefield. Stand firm for the principles—and the people—you believe in. Your flock does not need its caretaker to exhibit anxiety and fear.

7. *Sheep expect shepherds to be unselfish.* The president of a small chain of jewelry stores in Florida was under tremendous pressure from the board to slash overhead and produce a projected profit for the coming year. As much as he personally detested the decision, he was forced to eliminate the Christmas bonus his key employees were anticipating. "You've got to cut costs immediately," he was ordered. "It can't wait until next year!"

When the process was completed, the board presented the president with a check for $20,000—to thank him for balancing the budget. "I deeply appreciate your generosity," he told them, "but you need to know that tomorrow morning I will be dividing this with my staff—all of it."

The affinity between you and your associates can't be one-sided. People expect to participate in decisions that affect the quality, quantity, and climate of their work. It must be a partnership that also includes rewards. When one succeeds, all succeed.

8. Sheep expect shepherds to give them dignity. "We have 438 units of labor on the books right now," the director of human resources stated during her presentation to the executive committee of a Dallas bank.

"Wait just a minute," an executive interrupted. "When you talk about a 'unit of labor' are you referring to a real person?"

"Yes, sir. I am," the director answered.

"Then please start treating them like people. They are not units, numbers, or anything else!" he exclaimed.

Be lavish in treating people with respect and dignity. Work is about much more than labor—*it is about lives.*

9. Sheep expect shepherds to be sincere. I heard about a fellow who was flying from California to New York for a business meeting. During the flight he found a bug in his salad. That evening when he arrived at the hotel he wrote a hot letter to the airline to express his great displeasure.

When he returned to his office on the West Coast, a reply from an executive at the airline was waiting for him. The letter read: "Dear Sir: Your letter caused great concern to us. We have never before received such a complaint and pledge we will do everything within our power to ensure such an incident never happens again. It might interest you to know that the employees serving you have been reprimanded and the entire plane is being fumigated. Your concern has not fallen on deaf ears."

Needless to say, the man was impressed. Then he noticed an interoffice memo inadvertently stuck to the back of his letter, with this message: "Send this character the Regular Bug Letter."

Leadership can't afford to be artificial. It must be genuine and sincere.

10. Sheep expect shepherds to care deeply about them. If deep inside you don't truly respect and love people, it's time to resign from any post of responsibility that involves personal contact. As a librarian once told me, "There are certain individuals who are much happier when they are given a computer and an office in the corner of the building. They just don't know how to interact and show their concern for people."

Sheep want shepherds who are sensitive and responsive—to their personal and professional needs.

I once saw this sign posted on the employee bulletin board of a medical clinic: "People don't care how much you know until they know how much you care." It's good advice.

It's All about Love

For most of my life I believed what I had been told about the uncompromising, austere, legal edicts handed down by Moses—the "lawgiver."

I had to take a new look at the topic, however, when I was invited to attend a seminar by Samuel Shultz, professor emeritus of Old Testament at Wheaton College. The session was titled "Deuteronomy: The Book of Love."

At dinner that same evening, Dr. Shultz expanded on his theme. "Neil, one of the great misconceptions of our time is that people believe the Old Testament was about the law and the New Testament was about love."[2] He smiled and said, "They're *both* about love!"

It's true. When Moses, the shepherd of the children of Israel, descended from the mountain where the Almighty gave him two stone tablets inscribed with the Ten Commandments, Moses spoke to the people and declared, "And now, O Israel, what does the LORD your God ask of you but to fear the LORD your God, to walk in all his ways, to love him, to serve the LORD your God with all your heart?" (Deut. 10:12). And he added, "He defends the cause of the fatherless and the widow, and loves the alien, giving him food and clothing. And you are to love those who are aliens, for you yourselves were aliens in Egypt" (vv. 18–19).

We are to keep the law, and that is only possible through feelings that flow from the heart. "Love the LORD your God and keep his requirements, his decrees, his laws and his commands always" (Deut. 11:1). "Faithfully obey the commands I am giving you today—to love the LORD your God and to serve him with all your heart and with all your soul—then I will send rain on your land in its season" (v. 13).

What is the secret of keeping the law? Love!

REMINDERS FOR LEADERS WHO LOVE

- Demonstrate your concern for the security of others.
- Nurture people by being flexible and dynamic.
- Make it a habit to call your associates by name.
- Establish a reputation for being gentle and kind.

- Constantly show your interest in others.
- Be fearless in defending your flock.
- Build a partnership, not a kingdom.
- Treat every associate with dignity and respect.
- Be certain your actions are heartfelt and sincere.
- Show people how deeply you care.
- The great principles and laws can only be kept through love.

True leaders come to the realization that their sheep were not created to be sheared, or to be served as lamb chops or mutton stew. They are unique individuals who have great expectations about their shepherd.

It is a defining moment when someone in authority finally reaches the conclusion that leadership is not about *using* people—it's about *serving* them.

4

New Sight for Your Vision

■ Ken Lipke was a chiropractor in Buffalo, New York. He loved his city and was deeply saddened when, one by one, the giant steel mills closed their doors. The future of the community looked bleak.

"I didn't know much about industry," Ken told me as I was a guest in his home, "yet I knew plenty about the principles of success and believed they could be applied anywhere."[1]

Without any substantial finances, but endowed with enthusiasm and a vision, he formed an investment company and built Gibraltar Steel—which became one of the most profitable steel companies in the United States.

Says Lipke, "Before starting this venture I studied the lives of successful people and discovered there was a common thread." In reading their biographies he noticed that persistently cropping up were phrases such as, "I couldn't wait to get to the office every morning," or "It wasn't like work—it was more like a love affair." They not only had a dream, they became emotionally attached to it.

Lipke learned that finding people with technical skills and detailed knowledge of steel processing was easy. Qualified accountants, managers, and salespeople were abundant. But the ideas he learned from people like Robert Schuller and Norman Vincent Peale were his spark plugs. He developed the ability to build an atmosphere of optimism and teamwork that resulted in a giant corporation.

What was Gibraltar's rock? Love!

Checking Your Sight

What distinguishes an extraordinary leader from a run-of-the-mill manager? It is the ability to peek into the future and capture a picture worth pursuing. And something more. They are able to inspire others to join them in the quest.

On several occasions I have listened to my friend Leighton Ford share his mission in life—to invest his time and energy in the training of young world-changers. In his book *Transforming Leadership,* Ford says, "Vision is the very stuff of leadership—the ability to see in a way that compels others to pay attention."[2]

I can still remember watching President John Kennedy on television in 1961 declaring that the United States would "put a man on the moon by the end of the decade." That simple statement was more than pie in the sky; it was something average, ordinary citizens could envision. It also set the timetable for the space scientists at NASA that resulted in Neil Armstrong walking on the lunar surface July 20, 1969.

Evaluating a potential leader could easily include a trip to the optometrist. Is the person nearsighted or farsighted? The ability to see great distances is the most effective method for gaining the perspective required for achievement.

What is your reputation in your organization's environment? Are you seen as a visionary? Do they refer to you as a consensus builder? Are you someone who has "heart"?

Like a rising tide, a mental picture of possibilities lifts both your sight and your spirit. Ed Oakley and Doug Krug, in their book *Enlightened Leadership,* say: "Without a vision— an image of the way we want it to be—many of us tend to focus most of our attention on what's not working. By directing the energy toward correcting what is wrong with the present and focusing only on problems to be solved, we often lose sight of the ultimate objective in the process."[3] By nature, the visionary is a positive thinker.

You'll never reach your potential by becoming the organization's police officer. You must be much more concerned with reaching an objective than enforcing codes or micro-managing people's work schedules. A mortgage broker in Knoxville, Tennessee, told me, "Since we decreased the number of policies and increased the number of goals, there has been a noticeable increase in productivity around here."

How many times have you entered a restaurant to be greeted by a dour waitress or a grumpy manager? When it happens you usually mark the place off your map—even if the food was acceptable. People at every rung of the leadership ladder must fall in love with their work and approach it with enthusiasm and excitement. If you don't believe in what you are doing, your unhappiness will not only affect customers, it will infiltrate and impact every area of your life.

The biggest career mistake people make is to follow their skills rather than their heart. According to Barbara Sher, in her book *I Could Do Anything if I Only Knew What It Was*, "Relying on your skills to guide you is simply unacceptable. You should be doing what you love."[4] Says Sher, "What you love is what you are gifted at. Only love will give you the drive to stick to something until you develop your gift."

It's not what you can do, it's what you have a passion for that marks the difference between failure and achievement.

Building the Temple

The two things held in common by people who call themselves "happy" are: (1) they know exactly what they want in life, and (2) they feel they are moving toward achieving their objective.

Why is a clear vision so vital?

- It allows you and your associates to have a glimpse of a realistic future.
- It gives direction to everyone involved.
- It creates a mental image that shapes what is to come.
- It expands the boundaries and scope of your activities.
- It can energize virtually every element of an organization.

Have you ever read the story of the construction of Solomon's temple? It was a gargantuan task that involved seventy thousand carriers, eighty thousand stone cutters, and more than three thousand supervisors. If the same project were undertaken today it would still be considered a monumental venture costing untold sums.

It would be easy to conclude that King Solomon wanted to erect the greatest edifice in the world simply to create a legacy of honor and fame. However, that was not his objective. Solomon did not ask the Lord to give him riches or power; he asked for "a discerning heart to govern your people and to distinguish between right and wrong" (1 Kings 3:9). He envisioned the great temple as a way to honor God.

Solomon was a mighty leader, yet he had a tender heart. In one of his poems he penned these words: "Many waters cannot quench love; rivers cannot wash it away" (Song of Sol. 8:7).

The Master Plan

It's a great mistake to view leaders in terms of position. In truth, they exist everywhere, at every level of society—both inside and outside a corporation, in social circles, and among the self-employed. There is one common denominator. What is it? All real leaders have a compelling vision of the future.

After speaking at a seminar in Oklahoma, I had an enlightening conversation with a church business administrator. "Let me show you what we're working on," the man said excitedly as he pulled out an organizational chart that included more than seventy separate ministries of his church.

"You have all that going on? You must have a huge congregation," I commented.

"Oh, no," replied the administrator. "These are only our plans. Most of these slots aren't filled yet. It's our master plan for the next five years."

The staff of his church was practicing a proven principle of success—*seeing things not as they are, but as they are going to be!*

Perhaps you have visited a specially-constructed exhibit where a motion picture is projected on a 360-degree circular screen. You can see the action behind you, in front, and on all sides. That's the feeling you have as you begin to visualize what your organization can become. Suddenly you're absorbing the entire picture.

You may ask, "Is it necessary that my concept of the future be original? Do I have to create it from scratch?" No. For example, the manager of a furniture manufacturing company in North Carolina said, "I was reading the early history of our company and caught a glimpse of the passion for quality that was the driving force of the founders. From that moment I was determined that we would settle for nothing less than world-class craftsmanship in our factory."

Most important, whether the vision is original or handed down, you must buy into it, take ownership, and speak it into existence.

No one sees the exact same picture of the future. The film is always uniquely processed through the filter of our background and perspective.

I heard the story of four men who were gazing at a sunset in a national park in Utah. One of them was an artist and exclaimed, "This would make such a gorgeous painting. Just look at those dazzling hues!" Standing next to him was a geologist, who observed, "Isn't it fascinating how the sun is reflected against the rock formations in the mountains?" The third person present was a poet. He contemplated, "A setting sun always reminds me of the beautiful ending of one phase of our lives, and the beginning of another stage at sunrise." The final member of the group, a businessman, stared at the colorful sunset and blurted, "What a great view. I'd love to build a hotel right on this spot!"

The Write Stuff!

"I've got a big dream, yet nobody wants to help me achieve it," a young entrepreneur in South Carolina lamented. But he had never taken the time to write the vision clearly, and he had never presented it to anyone in a position to help make it a reality.

Take the time to place your dream on paper. Examine the words. Does it reflect what is in your heart? Will it inspire your associates? Scripture tells us to "write the vision, and make it plain . . . that he may run that readeth it" (Hab. 2:2 KJV).

Don't feel that your statement must be so definitive that no further explanation is necessary. John Kotter, in his excellent book *A Force for Change,* states: "Typically, a vision is specific enough to provide real guidance to people, yet vague enough to encourage initiative and to remain relevant under a variety of conditions."[5]

There is an art to striking the right balance between "fuzzy" and being graphic. When you allow your associates to help bring the picture into focus, they immediately feel part of the process.

When is the right time to pull back the curtain and allow others to hear what is on your heart? There may be an anniversary or major milestone to be celebrated by your organization. You may be about to launch a new product or make significant changes in your structure. Any of these moments may present the opportunity to talk about the future.

"I always wait until there is some kind of crisis in our company before sharing my vision," said the CEO of a telephone utility company in Pennsylvania. "At those moments people are extremely attentive and anxious to know there is hope for the future."

Be certain to place your concept in a realistic time frame. Your associates want to know, "When will we see the results?"

Don't depend on short-term solutions, however. People need to project ahead six months, a year, two years and more. They also desire to know what kind of rewards will be theirs if they embrace the dream.

Is your vision one that people will long to identify with? If they board the plane, do they know where they will be flying?

Can They See It?

During the Great Depression, Franklin D. Roosevelt swept into power with campaign slogans that included: "Two chickens in every pot. Two cars in every garage."

Those were well-chosen words people quickly adopted. The slogans were not a nebulous theory about what would happen in some distant locale; the pot was in their kitchen, and the garage was attached to their house.

When you build a future that allows people to reach *their* goals, they will instinctively help you in reaching *yours*. For example, you may be inspired to say, "We see the opportunity on the horizon to expand into Asia, Africa, and Latin America."

Your workers may reply, "So what? Does that mean I may get a free trip?"

If you want them to throw their weight behind the process, let them know that "by growing globally, we have the chance to secure our future and increase the benefits to all of our employees."

Never forget that the environment in which we work is much more than brick and mortar. At times it can be a highly emotional atmosphere. As a bookstore manager told me, "I have come to the conclusion that I not only need managerial skills to survive. There's also a spiritual element involved."

While some people work with data, technology, and physical materials, an effective leader is often moving the enterprise forward with ideas, concepts, and beliefs.

Great aspirations don't suddenly turn into reality simply because you speak the word. Ideally, the future you articulate will be a "working" vision. You will say, "It's going to take the creativity and personal enterprise of each of you to make this happen."

To have any chance of success, there must be a consensus on the goals and objectives from top to bottom. Without unity, your associates will simply be "going through the motions."

Communicate! Communicate!

You will learn that lofty plans can come crashing down if they are not constantly communicated. Once when I was involved in a regional development program for a nonprofit organization, a member of the executive committee told me, "Neil, the best advice I can give you is to create a monthly update and send it to every member of the board. There's no substitute for regular contact to keep the fires burning."

Organizational leaders Warren Bennis and Burt Nanus say: "A vision of the future is not offered once and for all by the leader and then allowed to fade away. It must be repeated time and again. It must be incorporated in the organization's culture and reinforced through the strategy and decision-making process. It must be constantly evaluated for possible changes in the light of new circumstances."[6]

If you want to expand the future, share it.

REMINDERS FOR LEADERS WHO LOVE

- Become emotionally attached to your vision.
- Involve others in your future.
- Learn the value of being farsighted.
- Don't become a micro-manager.
- Great leaders have tender hearts.
- Reduce your vision to a written statement.
- Choose words people will embrace.
- Set a realistic time frame for achievement.
- Create a "working" vision.
- Keep the fire of your dream burning.

Tomorrow will only be as great as the lives it will affect. That's what truly makes the process worth the investment of time and talent.

Is there a visionary on your team? Why not you?

5

Mission Number One

■ When Dr. Martin Luther King gave his moving "I Have a Dream" address in Washington, D.C., on August 23, 1963, he was painting a picture of the future he hungered to see. His words touched the hearts of millions as he repeated the theme again and again, communicating mental images such as: "I have a dream my four little children will not be judged by the color of their skin but by the content of their character."[1]

As we have been discussing, the proclamation of a vision is vital—and that was the core of King's message. Yet another step must be taken that determines the future of both individuals and enterprises. It involves the writing of a mission statement.

When it comes to leading with love, I know of no other document you can produce that makes the task more attainable. Why? Because it espouses your values and beliefs and becomes a blueprint for achieving your objectives.

Later in this book you will see how the difficult tasks of discipline and correction become much easier when the mission is the measuring stick.

You may ask, "What is the difference between a vision and a mission statement?"

- The vision is what you are striving to achieve and what you desire to be.
- The mission statement describes how you will live your life as you fulfill the vision. It gives a reason for being and becomes the foundation on which the future depends. The mission defines what is to be accomplished, not simply what is to be aimed for or pursued.

What we are discussing is older than you may think. The first statement of mission ever recorded was given by the Creator when he declared: "Be fruitful, and multiply" (Gen. 1:22 KJV). Today, the need for a firm, clear pronouncement of intent continues.

In 1989 Charles and Anne Winters launched the National League of Junior Cotillions, an etiquette and social training program with the objective of establishing chapters nationwide. "We knew that we wanted to have a positive effect on young people but were not quite sure how to communicate our purpose," says Charles, NLJC president.[2]

It was two years into the process before Charles and Anne and their team members began working on a statement that would define their mission. They settled on this phrase: "To learn to treat others with honor, dignity and respect for better relationships with family, friends and associates."

Continues Charles, "From the moment we settled on that statement it seemed to bring everything into focus and the organization experienced tremendous growth." NLJC, which has been featured by the major media networks, now trains thousands of students each year through hundreds of cotillion programs nationwide.

What Are Your Values?

Whether you are a schoolteacher or own a manufacturing plant, you are shaped by the principles and values you cherish.

ServiceMaster Corporation, one of the largest cleaning service conglomerates in the world, is serious about its objectives and beliefs. Kenneth Wessner, chairman of the board, says, "The philosophy of a company determines the character and nature of business it conducts. The climate of a company is created by the concepts of managing and life that govern its policies and practices." Adds Wessner, "The philosophy of ServiceMaster and the words we used to express that philosophy have been carefully conceived, nurtured, and refined through years of thought, work, and commitment. Our company philosophy is expressed in four objectives."[3] Here are the four statements the company is built upon:

1. To honor God in all we do.
2. To help people develop.
3. To pursue excellence.
4. To grow profitably.

What has been the impact of these principles? Many people at ServiceMaster say, "Our work is not merely the making of a living; it is a way of life."

When the objectives are precise and nonnegotiable, the burden of leadership lessens. Ken Blanchard and Michael O'Connor, authors of *Managing by Values,* make this observation: "In an organization that truly manages by its values, there is only one boss—the company's values."[4]

As the leader of any group, from a Boy Scout troop to an international trade association, your focus becomes clear when there is a stated purpose. For example, being the trustee of an organization simply means that you are keeping the mission of that organization in trust. As the president of a school board stated: "I view my role not as an ordinary responsibility, but a very sacred duty."

The document you create can effectively demonstrate the love and affection you have for those you serve. Part of the mission statement of Tom's of Maine, a firm that manufactures an all-natural line of personal care products, reads: "To respect, value and serve not only our customers, but also our coworkers . . . to be concerned about and contribute to their well-being, and to operate with integrity so as to be deserving of their trust. To acknowledge the value of each person's contributions to our goals, and to foster teamwork in our tasks."[5]

Those same heartfelt sentiments are reflected in the statement of a Texas air carrier. "The mission of Southwest Airlines is dedicated to the highest quality of customer service delivered with a sense of warmth, friendliness, individual pride and company spirit."[6]

The Process

Thousands of leaders can testify to the fact that preparing a statement that sets forth your values and beliefs can become a significant turning point.

When Corporate Child Care Management Services in Nashville, Tennessee, crafted its governing document, people from virtually all levels of the organization became involved in the endeavor. Says company president Marguerite Sallee, "I believe that the process of developing and refining a mission statement is as important as the statement itself."[7]

We all know how imperative it is for individuals to "buy into" a plan or program—whether it be the funding of a youth activities building or the remodeling of a company headquarters. If every decision is decided at the top, the chances of success are greatly diminished. How can we expect people to love the mission when they have had no part in creating it?

Here's an eight-step process for developing a mission statement that will be embraced by your associates:

1. Create a task force that represents individuals from all levels of your organization.
2. Set a target date for the completion of the process. (No less than six months.)
3. Define the eventual audience for your statement. Is it only for your team members? Is it for the general public?
4. Let small groups work on individual aspects of the eventual document and have them ask for input from everyone possible.
5. Have sessions where one or two elements of the statement are thoroughly discussed.
6. When the process is completed, decide how it will be distributed or published.
7. Celebrate changes the organization makes that reflect the implementation of the document.

8. Find ways to reward and honor associates who are demonstrating the spirit of the mission.

Remember, a vision must come from the heart of the leader. The statement that articulates that objective, however, needs to be the united effort of those it affects. That is what produces true *ownership*.

The result of such a process at St. Joseph's Hospital in Hamilton, Ontario, produced a "we" document that includes the following:

- We believe in the dignity of the person and the sacredness of human life.
- In response to the gospel message, we have a special obligation to the poor and unwanted.
- We communicate with our patients and each other openly, honestly, and with sensitivity.
- We respect patients' different needs in our multicultural and multilingual community.
- We expand the boundaries of health science by developing and promoting research activities.

At the end is an important note: "This Mission Statement reflects the contributions of 900 staff members of St. Joseph's Hospital."[8]

How long should the document be? There are no exact guidelines since the length is not as vital as the message it conveys. It may take three pages to define your purpose. Or, like Wendy's International, the fast food restaurant, only three words. Wendy's mission statement simply says: "Deliver total quality."

Make the aim and purpose of your organization as easy to communicate as possible. For example, John R. Corts, president of the Billy Graham Evangelistic Association, tells the world: "The mission of the BGEA is focused and simple: to support the evangelistic calling and ministry of Dr. Billy Graham to take the message of Christ to all we can using every means we have available."[9]

Make It Personal

You don't need to wait for a position of leadership to write your mission statement. It is a task every individual needs to embark upon early. Sadly, many wander through life without ever discovering and defining their intentions.

Begin by asking yourself these questions:

What is the primary objective and purpose of my life?
What values do I cherish?
What principles do I hold dear?
What are my beliefs?
How will I achieve my mission?
What will be the results of my actions?

As you weigh the words of your answers, a pattern will begin to emerge that will allow you to write and refine your statement. If you are not satisfied with your first attempt, don't panic. This is a working document that will likely undergo many revisions. In fact, you need to periodically review your intentions to be certain they continue to reflect the real you.

In Columbus, Ohio, a university student wrote: "My objective is to live with integrity and to make a difference in the lives of others." Then he listed the ways in which he would fulfill the task.

A successful real estate salesperson in Tennessee includes these words as part of her personal statement: "I, Pat Ford

Davis, have a mission in life to strive for and uphold in the highest regard the attributes I feel that necessitate a meaningful life for myself, my loved ones, friends and others. I am a person of integrity, honesty, and good moral character. I feel that treating others fairly will, in turn, cause others to act in like fashion."[10]

Resist the temptation to copy someone else's statement. It must be your own. Assign the highest priority to this endeavor and take your time crafting the document. What you eventually produce will be a "constitution" upon which you make daily decisions.

REMINDERS FOR LEADERS WHO LOVE

- Your vision reflects the destination. Your mission statement reveals how you will attain it.
- Take the time to write your values and beliefs.
- You are shaped by the principles you cherish.
- Allow your statement to be the guide for your decisions.
- Treat the mission as a sacred trust.
- Your document should mirror heartfelt feelings.
- The writing process can be as important as the finished product.
- Give your associates ownership by allowing them to contribute to the document.
- The length of the statement is not as important as what it conveys.
- Be certain the purpose is easy to communicate.

- Write your personal mission statement.
- How will you achieve your objective and what will be the results of your actions?
- Review both your organization and personal statements periodically.

What will be the ultimate outcome? As the executive of a volunteer organization stated, "You will have more than a sense of mission; you will be *on* a mission."

In a world that continues to swirl around us—often with gale-force winds—it is our purpose that provides the anchor.

Remember, your vision reflects where you are headed, your values indicate what you stand for, and your mission is your reason for being. Have you defined them?

6

The Qualities
of Leaders Who Love

■ There are people who will tell you, "Leaders are born,
not made!"

Don't believe them. There is nothing in your DNA or
genetic pattern that shouts, "Look out, world! Here comes
a real trailblazer!"

When you examine the backgrounds of those who command respect as leaders you will uncover a myriad of backgrounds—high school dropouts, housewives, musicians,
and Yale-educated lawyers. It makes no difference. Sure,
there are individuals who inherit their position because
of a powerful family, yet their ability to lead is not guar-
anteed. They are often replaced by someone who started
as a blue-collar worker and rose through the ranks.

Business gurus Warren Bennis and Burt Nanus make
this observation: "While *great* leaders may be as rare as
great runners, great actors, or great painters, everyone has

leadership potential, just as everyone has some ability at running, acting, and painting."[1]

Fourteen Qualities of Leadership

How can the promise become a reality? It happens when we deliberately adopt proven qualities. The specific characteristics of the person who makes a commitment to love-based leadership can be found in a letter written centuries ago by the apostle Paul. He told the people at Corinth, "Love is patient, love is kind. It does not envy, it does not boast, it is not proud. It is not rude, it is not self-seeking, it is not easily angered, it keeps no record of wrongs. Love does not delight in evil but rejoices with the truth. It always protects, always trusts, always hopes, always perseveres" (1 Cor. 13:4–7).

Those who embrace the fourteen qualities found in Paul's words will see a profound transformation—personally and in the lives they touch.

1. Leaders who love are patient. Have you ever met a farmer who can sow and reap on the same day? No. It takes watering, weeding—and waiting. The same holds true when you are growing *people.*

The director of development at a small college told me, "I'm not sure I would raise a dime if I pressured for a gift on the first call." He added, "It takes considerable time and effort to develop the kind of relationship that results in financial support. We expect people to have love for a cause, but they want to feel our care and concern for them as donors. And that doesn't happen overnight."

There's only one way to cultivate a lasting affinity and rapport with your associates. Plant plenty of seeds and never stop nurturing.

2. Leaders who love are kind. At a breakfast meeting with some friends a man asked, "If someone were to pay you ten cents for each kind word you ever spoke about others and collect five cents for each unkind word, would you be rich or poor?"

I hope I would be wealthy. The question, however, caused me to pause and consider that kindness is not only to be displayed in someone's presence but also in their absence. Caring must not be an act; it must be a lifestyle.

When people describe your qualities, what words are used? Let's hope they include *considerate, helpful,* and *thoughtful.*

3. Leaders who love are not jealous or envious. "She speaks from both sides of her mouth," complained the assistant to an insurance executive in Detroit. "One day she gives us a pep talk on the importance of teamwork and cooperation, then the next day she breaks into a temper tantrum when a colleague at her level receives a major promotion."

It has been said that if envy were a fever, all the world would be ill. Its effects are certainly devastating. It can rob you of your energy, misplace your focus, and keep you from accomplishing your vision.

Great leaders stay with their own agenda and don't become sidetracked by the success of others.

4. Leaders who love are not boastful or proud. A friend of mine likes to say, "You can always tell a leader, but you can't tell him much." Fortunately, that sentiment does not apply to those who are truly sensitive to the people they serve.

The office of authority is no place for smugness, pride—or those suffering from *I*-dolatry. Conceit is known as that strange disease that makes everyone sick except the person who has it.

It requires walking a fine line to be proud of your family and the success of your organization, yet at the same time be humbled by those same achievements. At every opportunity choose modesty over vanity and humility over conceit.

5. Leaders who love are not rude or ill-mannered. While making a phone call from a restaurant in Philadelphia I noticed a sign posted just inside the kitchen. It read: "Attention all employees. For every act of kindness, our customers will tell at least one friend. For every act of rudeness they will tell *ten!* We have made a business decision that on the third complaint of discourtesy or insolence you will be asked to look for employment elsewhere."

How can we reverse the tide of incivility that has swept our nation—from road rage to brazen acts of violence by children? We can begin with a personal decision that our conduct will be a role model of courtesy and respect.

6. Leaders who love are not self-seeking. A high school basketball coach who had been at the helm of the same team for more than twenty years was asked what it takes to win. "Our greatest seasons have been when we had average players who hustled as a team. The disasters came when we had a superstar who hogged the ball and attempted to put on a one-man show."

Psychologist James Dobson talked about this peril when he warned: "The philosophy of 'me first' has the power to blow our world to pieces, whether applied to marriage, business, or international politics."[2]

You will be surprised at what can evolve when you move the center of your universe from yourself to those around you.

7. Leaders who love are not easily angered. Last Christmas, at the exchange and refund desk of a department store in

Atlanta, a clerk posted a little sign that read: "Control yourself! Anger is only one letter short of danger."

We need to realize that our actions are generated from within, not because of outside forces. That means when you are about to lose your temper you can't blame the outburst on the way you were raised, the atmosphere where you work, or any other factor. You, and you alone, have the power to choose how you will react to circumstances.

The individual who decides to hold his tongue feels the same temptation as the one who blows his lid. What's the difference? A commitment to composure and self-control.

8. Leaders who love keep no records of wrongs and do not hold grudges. The pastor of an evangelical church near Orlando, Florida, had been leading the same flock for more than twelve years. Things were running smoothly except for the fact that one member, an influential banker, was constantly questioning his authority on business matters.

When the banker was nominated to become a deacon, the pastor stood before the congregation and said, "I don't believe this man is qualified to be elected." Then he read a long list of instances where the man had questioned the pastor's decisions.

Not only did the banker receive an overwhelming vote, the church began to view their minister in an unfavorable light. He resigned within six months.

A prime requisite for success is that you not only preach forgiveness, you practice it.

9. Leaders who love do not delight in evil. The owner of an automobile dealership in Southern California was tired of seeing full-page ads in the local paper advertising prices that were killing his sales. He became so desperate that he decided to make an offer to a young ad salesman he felt he could trust. "I'll buy two full pages every Friday and Saturday if you will confidentially fax me your other ad pages and extend me two hours past the deadline." The young man, anxious to increase his ad space, agreed and the dealer priced his cars as the lowest in the market.

Now there were two unethical culprits involved in deceit. Within six weeks questions began to be raised and the pressure on both men became so intense that the plan was quickly abandoned.

Never allow deception or dishonesty to gain the slightest foothold in your life.

10. Leaders who love rejoice in truth. What would be your reaction if you worked for an attorney who asked you to bill a client for four hours of legal work when you knew that not more than forty minutes had been devoted to the project?

You might feel your job was at stake and keep quiet. Yet there remains a sick feeling in the pit of your stomach and the respect you had for your employer begins to wane.

At every level of life, do your best to be transparent. Allow your associates to see your true character. Remember, strong bonds between people are not the result of written contracts and formal agreements. They are built on a strong foundation of truth.

11. Leaders who love are protective. My wife, Anne, was watering a fern hanging from a tree in our garden. Suddenly a bird flew nervously around her and she became frightened. When it happened the second time, she put down the watering container and looked closely at the fern. Cradled inside the foliage was a little nest with two tiny fledglings starting to emerge from their eggs. That mother bird had a natural instinct to care for her babies— and showed it by being extremely protective.

Here's a question every supervisor, manager, and executive needs to ask themselves: "Who has the most security in my organization? Me, or those I serve?" When you are committed to the safety and protection of others, you create the same results for yourself.

12. Leaders who love demonstrate trust. During the question-and-answer session of a seminar I was conducting in Hilton Head, South Carolina, a woman asked, "Why is it that so many people don't really trust their subordinates?"

I offered this suggestion: "Perhaps it's because they don't trust themselves!"

You do not need to have all the answers to motivate people. Just place your confidence in their abilities and turn them loose. That simple act can often produce greater results than all the instruction, discipline, and coercion you can muster.

The most powerful phrases in your arsenal should be these: "I believe in you." "I trust your decisions."

13. Leaders who love offer hope. A friend who is involved in a counseling center in Florida was asked, "Since you are involved in crisis counseling, aren't you discouraged by what you see and hear?"

He replied, "No! I'm *encouraged* because I have seen enough lives restored to know there is hope in any situation." He added, "Where there is great bondage, there can be great liberty."

How is hope communicated to your family, your friends, and to your team members? It occurs every time you talk about your vision—your positive view of the future. The more you share your heart, the stronger their faith and expectation will become.

A person needs just three things to be truly happy: Someone to love, something to do, and something to hope for. Is that what you are providing?

14. Leaders who love persevere. In the locker room of a high school gym, the athletic director painted this sign, "In the game of life nothing is less important than the score at halftime."

The trust, affection, and care you demonstrate to those around you can't be temporary. Those qualities must endure—through personal crisis, misunderstandings, economic reversals, and unexpected emergencies. You cannot afford to quit! Often it is the last key on the ring that opens the door.

Frank Wells, who sells printing franchises, tells his potential clients, "The secret to success is to start from scratch and keep on scratching."

Perseverance pays.

REMINDERS FOR LEADERS WHO LOVE

- Every person has the potential for leadership.
- Patience produces lasting results.
- Kindness must become a lifestyle.
- Don't allow envy to rob your vision.
- Choose humility, not conceit.
- Become a model of courtesy and respect.
- Replace being self-centered with being others-centered.
- Practice the art of self-control.
- Bury your grudges.
- Adopt a personal code of ethics.
- Build on a foundation of truth.

- Demonstrate trust in your associates.
- Offer a vision of hope.
- Allow your love to endure.

Paul, who presented the characteristics we have been discussing, adds these significant words: "If I have a faith that can move mountains, but have not love, I am nothing. If I give all I possess to the poor and surrender my body to the flames, but have not love, I gain nothing" (1 Cor. 13:2–3).

Are you demonstrating the qualities of love?

7

The Servant's Secret of Success

■ Many believe that the ability to lead is uniquely bestowed on those who are naturally gifted speakers, or individuals who have a special charisma. Such qualities may help, but the man or woman who reaches the top and *stays* there understands this seldom-practiced principle of achievement: *The power of leadership flows from the bottom to the top.*

Authority doesn't exist because a particular person happens to sit at the apex of an organization. Rather, governance is possible because there are people to govern.

- Without pupils, why would we need a teacher?
- Without a congregation, why would we need a minister?
- Without workers, why would we need a manager?

During every major election we see powerful senators, congressmen, and public officials thrown out of office because they were not responsive to the will of the people. And our entire legal system would be plunged into chaos if "common law"—the laws held by the majority of people—were not the basis of standards that rule society.

Is steel made from the clouds rising from the factory smokestacks? No. It is forged from the iron being melted in the fiery furnace below.

The manager of a tennis facility in Denver began greeting the receptionist each morning with, "Hello, Boss!"

At first she just smiled. Then, after hearing the same words for several days, she asked, "Why are you calling me *boss?*"

"Because you are," the manager replied. "Without you and every person here taking charge, I'd be sunk!"

The Japanese have a proverb that says, "If he works for you, you work for him." That sentiment was expressed by the manager of a plant in Indiana that produces lawn mowers. He posted this sign above the assembly line: "Where every leader works and every worker leads."

Great servants become great leaders because they understand the true source of power. As Sparky Anderson, former manager for the Detroit Tigers, once said, "No manager ever won no ball games."[1]

What Will You Remember?

People—especially those who produce goods rather than provide services—continue to ask themselves, "How can I find fulfillment in my work?"

The answer is rarely found in the quantity of the production or even in the quality of the end result. In the final analysis we're all in the *people* business.

Ten, fifteen, or twenty years from now you won't remember much about organizational charts, production quotas, or physical facilities. What you will recall are the heartwarming, personal comments of your associates.

During a leadership seminar in Illinois, I asked several participants to share the most rewarding experiences of their careers.

- One man told what it meant to speak at the funeral of a valued employee.
- Another shared the story of a former drug addict he had helped to become a productive manager.
- A woman unfolded a well-worn note from a fellow worker she carried in her purse—and she read it to the group. The note said, "If you ever get discouraged, remember that you have made a real difference in one person's life—mine!"

Do you see the pattern? What matters most are the relationships.

Perhaps you have heard the phrase "It's lonely at the top." Of course it is for those who have chosen to isolate themselves. However, the opposite is true for the man or woman who embraces the fact that power rises from the bottom to the top.

The Key to Greatness

Rank and status have no place in God's value system.

Two thousand years ago James and John came to Jesus and requested a special favor. "Teacher," they said, "we want you to do for us whatever we ask" (Mark 10:35).

"What do you want me to do for you?" he inquired (v. 36). They replied, "Let one of us sit at your right and the other at your left in your glory" (v. 37). The Lord answered, "To sit at my right or left is not for me to grant. These places belong to those for whom they have been prepared" (v. 40). Then Jesus made this profound statement: "Whoever wants to become great among you must be your servant, and whoever wants to be first must be slave of all" (vv. 43–44). Servant leadership works—in reaching objectives, in building relationships, and in receiving God's approval. It is not an option. It's a necessity.

Selfless Acts

Dean Ornish, a medical doctor at the University of California at San Francisco, believes that servanthood also plays a significant role in our personal well-being. Ornish, author of *Stress, Diet, and Your Heart,* says that many heart patients see themselves as isolated, which can lead to stress and more illness.

He encourages people to get involved in doing things for others. For example, he once asked two patients who disliked each other to do each other's laundry. Such selfless acts, Ornish believes, promote our ability to become well.

Learning the art of serving is easier when you see yourself as part of a team that wins—not caring who receives the credit. This is true in virtually every human endeavor, from medicine to music. Someone asked the conductor of a great symphony orchestra which instrument he considered the most difficult to play. The conductor pondered for a moment and said, "Second fiddle. I can get plenty of first violinists, but to find one who can play second fiddle with enthusiasm—that's a problem. And if we have no second fiddles, we have no harmony."

The Right Perspective

Unfortunately, many "big thinkers" are also big-headed. The person who links lofty vision with conceit is usually masking a lack of self-esteem. True achievers have an understanding of how small they really are in the scheme of things.

President Theodore Roosevelt loved to spend his summers on San Juan Island, in the waters north of Seattle, near Victoria, British Columbia. If you've been there, you know what a beautiful spot it is.

"Teddy" was a well-known lover of nature. One night, after an evening of conversation, he took a walk with his friend, William Beebe. They stopped and looked up at the vastness of the universe and were in awe of the Milky Way, the Big and Little Dipper, and the endless black sky. Finally, Roosevelt broke the silence and said, "Now, I think we are small enough. Let's call it a night."

That's the right perspective. When you finally realize your weakness you begin to find great strength.

Faithful with Little

There is a powerful message in the parable of the man who was about to depart for a journey. He called his servants and entrusted his property to them. To one he gave five talents of money, to another two talents, and to another one talent, and departed on his adventure.

What did the men do with the funds? The servant who had received the five talents immediately put his money to work and gained five more. The one with two talents also invested and doubled his money. However, the servant who had received the one talent dug a hole in the ground and hid his master's money.

When the owner returned to settle his accounts he was upset with the servant who buried the funds. To each of the two who had invested wisely, he said, "Well done, good and faithful servant! You have been faithful with a few things; I will put you in charge of many things. Come and share your master's happiness!" (Matt. 25:23).

Wisdom and prudence can bring a bountiful harvest.

What Are You Building?

Let met tell the story of Clyde the carpenter, who spent most of his life working for one contractor and felt it was time to retire. He hadn't saved or invested his money, but he thought he and his wife would somehow scrape by.

The man went to his boss and announced, "I'm too tired to build any more houses. I've decided to call it quits. I am going to retire."

A few days later the contractor met with Clyde and said, "Please. Would you reconsider and build one final house? I really need your supervision. Please."

After much coercion, the carpenter agreed and began working on his last project. However, his heart wasn't really in it. As a result, the workmanship was shoddy and the quality fell far below his usual standards. The house barely passed inspection.

On the last day of construction, the contractor gathered his employees together at the job site and asked the carpenter and his wife to be present. The boss announced, "As you know, this is Clyde's last day with us. He has been a faithful employee of our company for years, and we want to do something special to honor him. Clyde, this house you have built is not going to be sold. We are giving it to you and your wife as a gift for many years of faithful service. This is your retirement home—one I know you will enjoy for the rest of your days!"

Clyde had just learned the greatest lesson of his life.

You may be thinking, "The principles of servant leadership sound fine in theory, but how can I know if they work?"

I can only ask you to alter your present course and make a concentrated effort to practice these concepts. Long ago, the Italian astronomer Galileo stated, "You cannot teach a man anything. You can only help him discover it within himself."[2]

Take the advice of the apostle Paul: "Do nothing out of selfish ambition or vain conceit, but in humility consider others better than yourselves. Each of you should look not only to your own interests, but also to the interests of others" (Phil. 2:3–4).

Just imagine what the world would be like if everyone began to live by the motto of Rotary International: *Service above self.*

REMINDERS FOR LEADERS WHO LOVE

- Power flows from the bottom to the top.
- Without followers there can be no leaders.
- Fulfillment comes through people, not things.

- Rank and status have no place in God's value system.
- Winners must never worry about who receives the credit.
- Servanthood decreases stress and anxiety.
- Those who are faithful with little will be given much.
- Always view others as more important than yourself.

The famous Japanese Samurai warriors were told to "die before going into battle."

What did those words signify? It was a statement that these brave men were ready to enter a conflict without fear of the consequences. The most tragic outcome had already been accepted.

Leadership is rarely a life-or-death situation, yet ask yourself, "Am I totally committed to serving others?"

8

"I Believe in You"

■ Here are the five most powerful word combinations in the English language:

"Thank you."
"Would you, please?"
"What do you think?"
"I am proud of you."
"I love you."

What is the common denominator? The one word that links these persuasive phrases is *you!*

During a lunch break at a seminar, I was seated with four men who worked for different organizations. The conversation somehow drifted to styles of leadership and one executive proudly explained, "I've tried all kinds of approaches. Now I manage by the numbers."

"By the numbers?" another man responded. "You've got to be kidding."

"Is that so wrong?" retorted the first man, defending himself.

"Of course it is," came the reply. "Numbers are not just numbers! They're someone's productivity. They represent someone's sales effort. Numbers are somebody's paycheck."

A leader may be able to control time, budgets, and the physical environment, but their attempt to suppress people will usually backfire. Instead of being harnessed or controlled, team members need to be *released* to accomplish the task at hand. It happens in a four-step process:

First:	Provide the right training.
Second:	Make the objective clear.
Third:	Express your confidence.
Fourth:	Turn them loose!

The words every associate or staff member is waiting to hear are: "I have faith in you. I believe you can do it!"

A Seven-Step Plan

How can we instill faith and belief in those around us? How will they know we truly care? Here are seven practical ways:

1. Love people for who they are. "I'm having a difficult time trying to change my leadership style," the head of a community-based organization confided. His voice was rather gruff and he admitted that he usually barked orders to his subordinates.

Deliberately, I changed the subject. "Tell me about your family," I asked. He pointed proudly to the pictures of two handsome teens in silver frames on his office credenza. "I love those kids to death. They're my pride and joy."

"Well, do you bark at them?" I asked.

"Sure, when they need it. But it rarely happens," he replied, smiling.

After conversing about his children for a couple of minutes, I said, "Let me tell you a secret. If you treat your employees like your teenagers, you'd have that same loving relationship here at the office."

He began to grasp the concept that he was *raising employees*—with the goal of seeing them become leaders in their own right.

The key to a loving relationship between parent and child is this: You don't love your kids because of what they do but because of who they are.

When you transfer this principle to the workplace you will begin to value each associate for his or her unique contribution. In the words of a longtime popular song: "I love you most of all because you're you."

2. Discover the dreams of others. Over the years I have spoken to all kinds of audiences, from state government conferences to college convocations. I must admit, however, the most enthusiastic people I have ever encountered are those who attend the conventions of network sales organizations such as the Amway Corporation.

The phenomenal growth of multilevel marketing is largely the result of allowing people to pursue their dreams. As one person told me, "This has been the most liberating experience of my life. It's been a crash course in personal growth, and I feel the sky's the limit!" Even if an individual is only exposed to such an organization for a short time, the self-help principles they learn will endure for a lifetime.

"We should *never* pour cold water on anyone's dream," says Danny Cox, a supersonic flight test pilot and corporate trainer. "Being unenthusiastic, down-in-the-mouth, and generally nonsupportive is the fastest and most effective way to choke any hope of synergy and growth out of your people."[1]

Successful leaders don't go around shouting, "Listen! Here's what we want!" Instead they are inquisitive—always tapping into the ambitions and desires of those they serve. "What do you think should happen?" they want to know. "If the decision were yours, what would it be?"

According to James Kouzes, president of the Tom Peters Group Learning Systems, there is a great myth that portrays the leader as "a renegade, who magnetizes a band of followers with courageous acts. In fact, leaders attract followers not because of their willful defiance but because of their deep respect for the aspirations of others."[2]

3. Put "you first" into practice. How often do you pause to consider, "If I were in her place, what would I be thinking?" Or, "How can I see it from his perspective?"

We are encouraged from childhood to place others first, yet few seem to demonstrate this fundamental principle. Instead, we constantly attempt to make a good impression and in the process send the wrong signal.

Here's how you can solve the problem and win friends at the same time. Instead of trying to make a good impression, let the other person know they're making a great impression on you!

Reread that last sentence and absorb the power of that simple idea. For example, when someone tells you what they do for a living, show that you are impressed. Respond with, "That sounds exciting. How did you ever get into something like that?"

When you zero in on letting people know you are interested in them, they will warm to you automatically. It's a practical way to put the "you first" principle into action.

4. Offer people what they love. There are scores of methods used to persuade and inspire people. However, one strategy rarely fails. Find out what someone likes and send them running after it!

When you learn what others love, you hold the key to their success. For example, David Allison of St. Luke's-Roosevelt Hospital in New York, took a group of overweight children and asked them to name their favorite television program. Then he connected the power of the TV set to an exercise bicycle. To watch their desired show they had to pedal.

Allison didn't nag the kids to pedal or lose weight. He explains, "We just said, 'Here you go. For the TV to work, you have to pedal. See ya!'"[3]

These "pedalers" were compared to a control group who did not have the same motivation—and those who exercised to watch their favorite shows had a noticeable reduction in weight.

It is a great lesson in human behavior. When you find out what people truly want, motivation is a cinch.

5. Learn the art of recognition. Throughout my life I've observed dozens of people—from parents to company presidents—who control subordinates by either praising or blaming. The obedient are rewarded, the disobedient are punished.

What's the danger in this process? You are making value judgments about people based on their actions. For example, when you praise your child for presenting you with a special gift, you are really saying, "You are good because you gave me this present." However, you may also be saying, "You would be bad if you didn't give the gift."

Rather than giving praise, try giving *recognition*. Instead of implying, "You are a 'good person' for bringing me this box of candy," say, "Thanks so much for the candy. I really appreciate it." You've just recognized the individual for his action and have avoided making a value judgment.

You will do those around you a great favor by getting out of the praise-blame syndrome. Instead of constantly seeking approval, they will soon be making positive contributions because it is the right thing to do.

Don Nelson, author of *1001 Ways to Energize Employees*, believes you need to recognize people immediately. Says Nelson, "As soon as you see someone doing something good, tell them about it. There's no need to wait until the annual awards ceremony."[4]

6. *Express and demonstrate your gratitude.* There are a variety of ways to tell people they're doing a great job.

"I give them a raise," said the director of a day-care center. The money always helps, yet raises are often expected and don't convey much meaning. In today's environment, people desire more.

Try these additional ways to say "thanks."

- *Thank people personally*—give a one-to-one expression of appreciation.
- *Thank people publicly*—they may pretend to be embarrassed, but they love the applause.
- *Thank people on paper*—there is nothing quite like the impact of something you have personally written.

Your gratitude doesn't need to be elaborate or expensive. It can be as simple as a handwritten note or a message sent by e-mail. One manager makes it a habit to read positive letters received from customers at staff meetings.

The Marriott company has operated with the belief that if employees are content, confident, and generally happy with themselves and their job, their positive attitude will make the desired connection. Says J. W. Marriott Jr., chairman and CEO of Marriott International, "We have countless associates who have demonstrated remarkable personal generosity and kindness toward guests over the years—stuff that no SOP (standard operating policy) can cover." He adds, "If those associates didn't feel terrific about themselves, I don't think they would be able to do some of the things they've done."[5]

Marriott gives these examples:

- Some have loaned money out of their own pockets to guests who forgot their wallets.
- Others have played emergency baby-sitter, ordered (and picked up) replacement contact lenses, and put their weekend mechanic skills to work on conked-out cars.
- Associates have loaned shoes, jewelry, coats, blouses, and other items to guests who didn't pack them.

That is going beyond the call of duty!

7. *Believe in yourself.* It is only when we are able to love ourselves that we are able to love others.

We are not talking about self-glorification. I'm sure you have met those who constantly toot their own horn and brag about their exploits. In most cases, these individuals are masking their insecurity and lack of confidence.

Others are narcissistic—enamored by their own appearance. The word is derived from a character in

Greek mythology named Narcissus. He saw his image reflected in the glassy waters and was captivated with himself.

The self-love necessary to lead people is based on assurance and the certainty that comes with self-respect and personal dignity.

- You learn to trust others by trusting yourself.
- You learn to be kind to others by being kind to yourself.
- You learn to have faith in others by having faith in yourself.

Self-esteem expresses itself through our relationships. According to noted psychiatrist Dr. Karl Menninger, "You cannot really love yourself and do yourself a favor without doing other people a favor, and vice versa."[6]

When you have developed an inner peace and confidence, here's what you will communicate without saying a word: "I believe in you because I believe in me."

It's a Partnership

One afternoon in Florida I was meeting with several people who were in charge of the direct-mail fund-raising efforts of a nonprofit organization. "We need to stop for a moment and reflect on what it means to be a partner," said one woman. "If we expect people to support us we must become their *equals,* not their superiors."

When we truly believe in people we will treat them as we want to be treated—with admiration and respect.

REMINDERS FOR LEADERS WHO LOVE

- Demonstrate confidence in those around you.
- Love people for who they are.
- Discover the dreams of others.
- Put "you first" into practice.
- Offer people what they love.
- Learn the art of recognition.
- Express and demonstrate your gratitude.
- Believe in yourself.
- Treat people with admiration and respect.

Climbing the love ladder is a dangerous assent without total faith and trust in those we serve. Tell someone today, "I believe in you!"

9

Abandon Yourself!

■ "You have the heart of an athlete," my doctor told me during my annual checkup. "Your EKG is perfect and you have a resting heartbeat of 59."

Two weeks later, however, pushing the lawn mower in my yard, I felt a sharp pain across my back. "What could that be?" I wondered, stopping for a few minutes to rest. When the pain eased I started the mower again and immediately the pain returned.

On Monday morning I was back at my physician's office. "Doctor, I think you'd better check me again."

When I described my symptoms he picked up the phone and scheduled a stress test with a cardiologist. I not only flunked the test, but the pain was extreme. Before the day was over I was given a heart catheterization that revealed three major blockages in my arteries—two were 80 percent blocked and one was 99 percent blocked.

"Neil, we have you scheduled for a triple bypass operation on Wednesday," my physician informed me.

"No problem," I responded. "If that's what I need, let's go for it!"

Looking back on the experience, I realize that my family and friends were much more concerned about the operation than I was. My attitude was: "This is beyond my control. I'm leaving it in the hands of God and the team of experienced heart surgeons."

In those eventful days I had a chance to put into practice a message I had preached for years—*abandon yourself to the strength of others!*

Total Reliance

The surgery was a textbook case and within weeks I was in a rehab program that changed my eating and physical fitness habits for life. At every step of the journey I met doctors, nurses, nutritionists, and physical therapists who were total professionals. And since they knew much more about their specialties than I, I simply relaxed and followed their advice.

Why be devastated by worry and anxiety when there is plenty of help available? Years ago I saw this phrase on the wall of an insurance company: "Cancer is curable. The fear of cancer is fatal." This also applies to heart patients.

The principle of reliance not only reduces self-doubt and fear, it endows you with unexpected strength. When you allow others to contribute their talent and expertise, you can focus your time and energy on building your own. When I spoke to my physician about the heart specialist he recommended, I didn't ask, "Is he a writer or a public speaker?" No. I wanted to know his reputation as a surgeon.

Recognize Diversity

One of my favorite books is *Leadership Is an Art* by Max DePree, the executive of a furniture manufacturing company in Michigan. I agree with his theory that when we truly believe in the potential of people, they rarely disappoint us. In his organization DePree demonstrated what it meant to totally rely on the strength of others. Says DePree, "Recognizing diversity gives us the chance to provide meaning, fulfillment, and purpose, which are not to be relegated solely to private life any more than are such things as love, beauty, and joy. It also helps us to understand that for many of us there is a fundamental difference between goals and rewards."[1]

What a liberating feeling it is to admit we have personal limitations—that we can't know everything or perform every act.

- Great parents take pride when their accomplishments are far surpassed by a son or daughter.
- Great teachers realize that even the youngest students have life experiences different from their own.
- Great leaders stand aside when they see talent rising to the top.

Seven Keys

Empowering those around you is like stretching out in a hammock. You place all of your weight—and your faith—in something you believe will hold you firmly. You are convinced it will not let you down.

Here are seven ways to practice the art of abandoning yourself to the strength of others.

1. Never be threatened by people with potential. I am sure you've encountered individuals who are threatened by subordinates. They are intimidated by people with creative ideas, jealous of those who are popular, and distance themselves from those they perceive to be intellectually superior.

Wise leaders don't see competition, only competency. When they recognize ability, they latch onto it quickly.

Amos Hostetter, founder of Continental Cablevision, one of the largest cable operators in the country, says his success is based on "finding the best people possible, even if they are potentially better than I am. I don't care. I want to find them, identify them, put them in place, give them the authority to make important decisions that really impact the value of this company, manage their careers so they experience every part of what we do, and make their compensation so attractive that they would never consider going anywhere else."[2]

2. To demonstrate trust, delegate. My first job after college was as program director of a new television station that was about to go on the air. I had a master's degree in broadcasting from Ohio State University, yet I was extremely nervous about the assignment. To my amazement, the boss called me into his office the first week and said, "Neil, I'm really counting on you. The program schedule is in your hands. I am trusting your judgment."

Wow! Those words gave me more confidence than you can imagine. Somebody *believed* in me—and I worked tirelessly to be worthy of that trust.

3. Look inside for advice. One of the great mistakes made by leaders in both large and small organizations is to rely on consultants. They spend thousands on fees and expenses to fly in so-called "experts" who know little about the enterprise and even less about its people.

In almost every case, the *real* experts in a school, a church, or a business are just a few feet away. If given the opportunity, the average employee can suggest solutions to nearly every issue faced by their organization. Start tapping this reservoir of potential.

4. Practice "progressive empowerment." What's the key to finding hidden talent? Begin by telling an associate, "I have a project I'd like you to work on." Then go one step further. Give that person the authority to act on your behalf. You will never know what an individual is capable of until you turn them loose. In most cases their efforts will be a pleasant surprise. Then, as they prove themselves, give them wider authority and greater tasks.

When leadership emerges, the organization automatically grows. It happens *progressively.*

5. Walk in the shoes of someone else. If you plan to use the expertise of others, you'd better know their values and their vision. It results from building more than a surface friendship.

After speaking at a banquet for hospital auxiliary volunteers in Missouri, I asked the administrator how she made the assignments for dozens of "free" helpers. "I spend several hours and sometimes *days* with each person before they are permanently placed," she told me. "I learn why they want to help and what their personal interests are." The result is a loyal, dedicated volunteer staff that provides an invaluable service.

Why not step outside of your shoes? Learn what is important to someone else.

6. Forget the secrets. How can you develop trust if you operate in a cocoon of confidentiality or secrecy? Teamwork requires transparency.

If your objective is to raise leaders, give every associate as much information as possible. That means frequent, open discussions on issues that matter. It requires that rumors be dealt with immediately. It demands honest conversations taking place between people at all levels.

7. Declare, "We're in this thing together." In Japan there is a well-known saying: "We all eat from the same pot." It's true. If the bowl becomes empty, everyone from the secretary to the president goes hungry.

For sheer survival, there is often no other option than to place our trust in the abilities of others.

They Finally Listened

Charles Farkas and Philippe De Backer, in their book *Maximum Leadership,* relate the story of a young college graduate who, forty years ago, joined a Japanese company as a clerk in a small department. He applied himself faithfully and went one step further. He often contacted corporate headquarters to point out deficiencies in the organization—and offered suggestions for correcting them.

For ten years his ideas were rarely acknowledged and never acted upon. Then one day as he was leaving work, he was stopped by an executive from corporate headquarters who had tracked him down. A few minutes later he was ushered into the president's office—a place he had never been. In that meeting he was informed that one of his suggestions was about to be implemented. The president expected it to save an entire division from bankruptcy. A few months later, it did!

The story doesn't conclude there. The young clerk eventually became chairman of the firm that once ignored his phone calls and notes. Because of his leadership, the culture of the organization has changed. Today, individuals who challenge the status quo are encouraged, even celebrated. The enterprising company is Canon—the multi-billion-dollar maker of cameras, copiers, printers, and fax machines.[3]

Water on the Sand

Alexander the Great, the Greek king, once led his troops across a desert. After nearly two weeks of marching, he and his soldiers were near death from thirst, yet Alexander forged ahead.

In the noonday sun, two of his scouts brought what little water they were able to find. It barely filled a cup. Alexander's troops were shocked when he poured the water into the burning sand. The king said, "It is of no use for one to drink when many thirst."

Treating those in your group or organization as "team members" or "associates" will not work if it's only a scheme or a strategy. Do you truly see them as equals? Is the word *partner* a genuine expression? Would you drink while many are thirsty?

In the words of the apostle Paul, "Do nothing out of selfish ambition or vain conceit, but in humility consider others better than yourselves" (Phil. 2:3).

REMINDERS FOR LEADERS WHO LOVE

- Practice the principle of total reliance.
- Don't be threatened by people with potential.
- To demonstrate trust, delegate.
- Look inside for advice.

- Practice "progressive empowerment."
- Walk in the shoes of someone else.
- Forget the secrets.
- Declare, "We're in this thing together."
- See every associate as an equal.

Amazing things happen when we begin to treat people as peers rather than subordinates. Carrying a heavy load becomes possible when the burden is balanced and the weight is evenly distributed.

Starting today, allow yourself to experience the surprising strength of others.

10

The Surprising Truth about Team Building

■ "This is one of the greatest challenges I've ever faced," the director of a recreation facility in Illinois told me. "I'm trying to form work teams throughout our staff, and it just isn't happening."

The longer we talked, the more I realized that his entire premise for building teams was misguided. "I've tried grouping people by age, by length of employment, by their personal interest, and by their experience," he continued. "And nothing seems to bring results."

"Of course not," I told him. "Teams don't work because of conformity; it's *diversity* linked by a common vision that creates the magic." That's the surprising truth about team building.

The Ultimate Task Force

An error often made by an inexperienced leader is to appoint a committee. Why? They tend to outlive their usefulness and are almost impossible to disband. There's something permanent about the word *committee*.

Another danger is that a tight-knit group with continuity can form both a clique and a negative power base within the organization. And that spells trouble with a capital "T."

Instead, form a "task force" to tackle one specific problem. And when the project is completed, issue a "cease and desist" order.

In my opinion, the ideal task force would have five or six members—each bringing a unique gift to the table. Here are the types of individuals I would choose:

1. **A knowledgeable person**—someone who has vast amounts of data on the topic to be addressed.
2. **A logical person**—a clear thinker who can organize the work of the group quickly.
3. **A creative person**—someone who will bring inspiration and innovation to the job at hand.
4. **A technical person**—the one who will address the inevitable computer issues.
5. **A person with great integrity**—someone with high ethical values who will add character and substance to the discussions.
6. **A communicator**—the person who will either write the report or become the spokesperson for the group to the larger community.

What is the driving force that channels the energies of people with such varied skills? It is the vision of leadership and the mission of the immediate objective. Stuart Levine, CEO of Dale Carnegie & Associates, says we should treat people like the unique creatures they are. "When individuals come together as a team, their individuality doesn't suddenly evaporate. They still have different personalities. They still have different skills. They still have different hopes and fears. A talented leader will recognize those differences, appreciate them, and use them to the advantage of the team."[1]

What Can You Do?

How do you inspire people to work *with* you rather than *for* you? What can you do to foster shared efforts, common goals, and mutual respect? Here are twelve strategies for transforming individual performers into team players:

1. Eliminate organizational charts. Names in boxes that show the flow of power only impress those at the top. Instead, create *relationship charts* with arrows that demonstrate how people interact with others at every level.

2. Become a coach rather than a boss. See yourself as a facilitator that inspires and releases the talents of your associates.

3. Stop controlling people and start empowering them. After a great military victory, it's not the general who has won, but the army.

4. Actively involve people in the decision-making process. Sure you can make decisions on your own—and that may be what your board expects. However, it's not the way to build a team. When you ask for input from associates you not only gain their goodwill, you may find some fresh ideas!

5. *Allow people to discover answers for themselves.* If you think you know the quickest and best solution, hold your fire. It's in self-discovery that people take ownership. See yourself as a guide, leading others in the right direction.

6. *Recognize and reward every team member.* In the National Basketball Association there is a "Sixth Man" award. It goes to a player who comes off the bench and makes an outstanding contribution to the team. The message is clear: *Every person is valuable, not just the starters.*

7. *Instead of centralizing authority, distribute it.* Transfer power to a relationship rather than a position. Trade micromanaging for vision-based leadership.

8. *De-emphasize rules and regulations.* Let the "Policies and Procedures" manual be rewritten by a task force that represents all associates. The results will be "our" guidelines.

9. *Create a nonintimidating atmosphere.* Allow people to offer ideas or criticism without feeling threatened. The intimidator asks, "Why did you choose that solution?" The team builder asks, "What do you think we need to do?"

10. *Continually ask for assistance.* One of the most important phrases in your vocabulary should be, "Will you help me?" It immediately lets people know how valuable you consider them to be.

11. *Adopt the "I need you" philosophy.* Do you remember the Lone Ranger? He needed Tonto, his faithful Indian scout, to give him directions. In the words of an old proverb, "Help your brother's boat across, and your own will reach the shore."

12. *Truly love your associates.* Legendary coach Vince Lombardi said, "I don't necessarily have to like my associates, but as a man I must love them. Love is loyalty; love is teamwork."

New Objectives

When an executive of the Gibraltar Steel Company in Buffalo, New York, gave me a tour of the plant, he pointed to a chart near the production line. "Years ago we measured and compared the productivity of individuals, but no more. It doesn't work," the man told me. "This chart compares our output and quality with previous time periods. If it increases, everyone shares the rewards."

Those at every level of management at Gibraltar credit the remarkable growth of the company to the team spirit that pervades the operation.

Stephen Covey, author of *The Seven Habits of Highly Effective People,* worked for several years with a large real estate organization. He recalls attending his first marketing rally where more than 800 sales associates gathered for the annual reward program. Covey describes it as a "psyched-up cheerleading session" with high school bands and plenty of screaming.

What struck him about the event was that only 40 of the 800 present received awards for top performance—including "Most Sales," "Greatest Volume," "Highest Earned Commissions," and "Most Listings."

Covey and his associates noted that while 40 people had won, 760 had lost. Since their mission was to spur sales, the next year 1,000 were present and over 800 were rewarded. How was it possible? *They developed a program for people to be awarded for self-selected performance targets and groups achieving team objectives.*

It worked!

Positive Peer Pressure

My friend Dave Scholl, owner of Construction Management in Charlotte, North Carolina, doesn't have difficulty motivating his team members. Periodically he has the workers in his home remodeling company anonymously evaluate fellow employees with whom they have worked for a period of two weeks.

On a scale of 10 (Excellent) to 1 (Very Poor) Scholl asks them to place a number before these twenty statements:

1. Has a good overall attitude.
2. Has a positive attitude toward the customer.
3. Has a positive attitude toward fellow workers.
4. Has a positive attitude toward the company.
5. Has a positive attitude toward work.
6. Tries to produce quality work.
7. Uses time wisely.
8. Interested in learning more about the trade.
9. Arrives at work on time.
10. Works at a positive rate of speed.
11. Seldom complains.
12. Does not try to find fault with other workers.
13. Is neat about cleaning up.
14. Returns borrowed tools.
15. Never uses abusive language on the job site.
16. Willingness to help fellow workers.
17. Tries to work well with subcontractors.
18. Is a team player.
19. Is organized about his work.
20. If you were the owner of your own company, would you hire this person?

Scholl told me, "It's incredible how this simple evaluation increases both quality and productivity."

It's easy to see why the questions are effective. The employee understands, "If I'm being asked about others, they're being asked about me." As a result, every day each worker is thinking about his attitude, professionalism, and interaction with others. Those who believe in isolation are whistling in the wind. As British economist Charles Handy wrote in *The Hungry Spirit*, "Almost everything we do affects other people, whether it is the pollution from our car or the decision to buy one company rather than another. National boundaries can't control the winds that carry acid rain, the flows of money, or the messages on the Internet. In no way can we stand alone and pretend that what we do affects no one else and that no one else affects us."[2]

The principles of teamwork were at the center of the apostle Paul's formula for spiritual success. He made this appeal: "That all of you agree with one another so that there may be no divisions among you and that you may be perfectly united in mind and thought" (1 Cor. 1:10).

REMINDERS FOR LEADERS WHO LOVE

- Unify diversity through a common vision.
- Eliminate organizational charts.
- Become a coach rather than a boss.
- Stop controlling people and start empowering them.
- Actively involve people in the decision-making process.
- Allow people to discover answers for themselves.
- Recognize and reward every team member.
- Instead of centralizing authority, distribute it.
- De-emphasize rules and regulations.
- Create a nonintimidating atmosphere.

- Continually ask for assistance.
- Adopt the "I need you" philosophy.
- Truly love your associates.

What are the benefits of team building? People feel they are making a positive contribution to the cause. Their satisfaction level zooms, creativity is renewed, and productivity increases. With excitement, they tell their friends, "Finally, I am being recognized for who I am."

It is impossible to place a value on the synergy produced by people who feel needed, accepted, and loved.

11

The Power of Cooperative Thinking

■ "We're about to have some exciting competition," said the manager of a steel plant in Ohio. "We have three eight-hour shifts and I'm going to issue this challenge. The shift that produces the most steel with the highest quality over the next thirty days will receive a substantial bonus for every worker."

For the first few days there was a lot of bantering between the workers as they changed shifts. "You just wait. We're going to win this thing," one night supervisor said to the incoming morning employees. It began as a friendly rivalry.

As time passed, however, what the manager thought was a great motivational device proved to be a disaster. Just a few days after the competition began, discord surfaced between the teams. For example, as one shift was about to leave the plant they would turn off the power so that the next group would have to refire the furnaces—losing precious time and producing less steel.

Workers in another shift dumped foreign materials into the furnace that would lower the quality of the steel for the next team.

At the end of the month, management was stunned. There had been a *decrease* in output.

Internal competition rarely works. It pits worker against worker, resulting in lower morale, diminished production, and friction in the organization. The lesson learned in that Ohio plant is one we all must discover sooner or later. We win through cooperation, not competition.

Where's the Competition?

Leaders in government, education, and business eventually come to the conclusion that you cannot compete externally if you compete internally. Let the contest be between your team and those who are far removed in time and space.

- America *should* compete with Japan in computer technology.
- Notre Dame *should* compete with Nebraska in football.
- Pepsi *should* compete with Coca-Cola for soft drink dominance.

However, creating rivalries between team members of the same school or organization is often a destructive force that makes more enemies than friends. Can you really expect ten computer salesmen to get along when they are each trying to win a trip to Cancun by making "Top Producer of the Month"?

Cooperation works because mutual goals promote trust, encourage communication, and decrease the fear of exploitation. The skills we acquire in the process of becoming a team player are remarkable. We learn to wear the hat of an arbitrator, a judge, a negotiator, and a fence mender. And we are constantly faced with the question: Is it fair to all concerned? It's been said that you cannot sink someone else's end of the boat and still keep your own afloat.

It Starts Early

The problems associated with competitive thinking start early.

My friend Charles Dygert, author of *Success Is a Team Effort,* says, "If you didn't encounter a domineering, autocratic environment in your home, you probably did when you entered first grade. It was there you more than likely faced the stark reality of a competitive world. You were thrown into a rivalry with other pupils, and for many it was where serious problems began."[1]

Behavioral research tells us that at the age of five we still have most of our natural creativity, but by the time we are seven we may have only ten percent of it left. The theory is that in the first grade we become regimented. Our freedom to play is suddenly stifled and cooperation greatly decreases. We are given specific tasks to learn—and we are told to learn them alone. Through years of education, we are given thousands of hours of homework assignments. Are they team projects? No. We are expected to do the work by ourselves.

Every leader needs to understand that more effective learning takes place through collaboration than working alone. For example, when students are charting their own course and devising ways to make the top grade on an exam, there are achievers and failures. On the other hand, when teams of students work together on a problem, exceptional learning and social interaction takes place. Everybody wins.

Marcus Aurelius said, "We are made for cooperation—like feet, like hands, like eyelids, like the rows of the upper and lower teeth. To act against one another is contrary to nature."[2]

Only a small percentage of people function well in an environment where they are forced to compete with their associates.

Henry Ford was the first to build an "assembly line" to produce great numbers of automobiles. However, he didn't take a mass-production approach to his employees. Ford, known as a great storyteller, spent a great deal of time in friendly chitchat with the staff—from hourly workers to managers. And his greatest leadership skill was avoiding the phrase, "I want this done." Instead, he would ask, "I wonder if we can do it?"

Your Personal Best?

During a question-and-answer session at a teachers' seminar in Dallas, the principal of an elementary school was asked, "Sir, I'd like you to talk about the concept of striving to achieve your personal best."

He paused for a few moments and said, "I can't tell you about my personal best."

"Why?" asked the questioner.

"Because it wasn't me. It was *us.*"

Remember, you don't have to be a specialist in multiple skills to be a success. The gap between what you lack and what you need can quickly be filled when you embrace the gifts of others. When you cooperate—and don't care who takes the credit—the results can be amazing.

I like the attitude expressed by former NBA player Ron Hundley. Recounting his career, he said, "My biggest thrill came the night Elgin Baylor and I combined for 73 points in Madison Square Garden. Elgin had 71 of them!"

Communicate!

In 1970, Tom and Kate Chappell began a company to produce personal care products made with natural ingredients. They also believed the organization would thrive if the atmosphere was one of harmony rather than rivalry. The firm, Tom's of Maine, has become a great success story.

In his book, *The Soul of a Business,* Tom states, "When people who work together step beyond the niceties of office chitchat and indulge in some real conversation that allows them insight into each other's lives, it enriches the experience of going to work." And he adds, "Any boss who gives people a reason to love going to work is going to see results in productivity that he's going to love."[3]

Cooperation is fostered by constant communication.

Terry Paulson, author of *They Shoot Managers, Don't They?,* tells about a top executive at a large computer firm who had a bridge-building strategy with his fellow employees. The man told him, "An executive corner office may give you a great view, but it doesn't give you the people contact you need."[4]

By arranging to have an office near the rest rooms, he was assured of seeing everyone he needed to influence at least two or three times a day. It also gave him a way of handling the long-winded ones. Laughs Paulson, "He'd catch them on the way in."

Lessons from Lions

What are the results of cooperative thinking? Let me share these two stories about the "king of the jungle."

In West Africa they tell a story about a young lion and a panther. The animals were both very thirsty and arrived at a small watering hole at the same time. Immediately they began to bicker over who had the right to drink first. The contest became heated, and each said, "I'd rather die than surrender my rights to use this watering hole first."

Instead of quenching their thirst, they soon were savagely clawing and biting each other. Their wrath continued until blood began to flow.

Suddenly, because of what was happening above them, the lion and the panther stopped fighting. Overhead was a circling flock of vultures waiting to see who would fall to the ground first. Instead, the lion and the panther outwitted the vultures. They drank from the water at the same time and walked off together in harmony.

Whatever your objective, make certain you know who the real opponent is.

The second story is one of Aesop's fables. He wrote about a lion who was sleeping in the sunshine when a little mouse ran across his paw and awakened him. The great lion trapped the little rodent and was about to have a snack. The mouse cried, "Oh, please, let me go, sir. Some day I may help you." The lion scoffed at the idea that the tiny mouse could be of any practical use to him.

However, he was a good-natured lion and set the mouse free.

A few days later the lion became ensnared in a large net. He tugged and pulled with all his might, but the ropes were far too strong. He roared loudly—and that little mouse heard him and ran to his rescue.

"Be still, dear Lion, and I will set you free," insisted his tiny friend.

With his sharp little teeth, the mouse gnawed through the ropes and the lion escaped from the net. "Once, you laughed at me," said the mouse. "You thought I was too small to help you. But see, you owe your life to me."

To whom will you turn for help?

REMINDERS FOR LEADERS WHO LOVE

- Competition should be external, not internal.
- Rivalries between associates can lower morale and diminish production.
- Mutual goals promote trust.
- Teamwork fosters healthy communication.
- We must ask, "Is it fair to all concerned?"
- Cooperation protects us from outside danger.
- We win through cooperation, not competition.

There is a great message in these words from the Old Testament: "Two are better than one, because they have a good return for their work: If one falls down, his friend can help him up. But pity the man who falls and has no one to help him up! Also, if two lie down together, they

will keep warm. But how can one keep warm alone?
Though one may be overpowered, two can defend them-
selves. A cord of three strands is not quickly broken"
(Eccles. 4:9–12).

Start cooperating!

12

Replacing the Culture
of Conflict

■ A network broadcasting executive, speaking before a group of writers, said, "If you want to have high ratings for a television show, you'd better include the one essential ingredient—conflict!"

It's true. That is what attracts large audiences to game shows, soap operas, dramatic films, and the network news. For dozens of hours every week we are subjected to story lines that involve tension, friction, and serious confrontation.

Unfortunately, the strife is not limited to television, movies, or the headlines of our morning newspaper. There is a serious upturn in violence and rage throughout society—between children and parents, students and teachers, employees and bosses.

Researchers at the University of North Carolina business school interviewed 1,200 workers and found that 52 percent of the respondents who were on the receiving end of rude behavior said they lost time worrying about it. Of the workers 22 percent deliberately decreased their productivity and work effort. And 12 percent actually quit their jobs to avoid the perpetrator.[1]

Outside the office, there is growing rage among airline passengers, customers in restaurants, and drivers on our nation's highways. Last year more than two thousand violent incidents resulting from "road rage" were formally reported by police nationwide. I'm sure you've seen people yelling at other drivers, honking, blinking bright lights, revving their engine, making insulting gestures, following too close, and "cutting off" another driver.

Many trace the roots of the current problem to the late 1960s. Toward the end of the Vietnam War a tidal wave of antiestablishment protests swept across America. I can remember the change in student behavior at a private college campus. They hung the president of the school in effigy simply because it was snowing outside and he wouldn't dismiss classes.

From those momentous days until the present, people have been demanding their "rights" and attempting to exert control with alarming boldness. As a high school football coach recently stated, "We formed a booster club, but by the end of the season it had turned into a terrorist group!"

Emotional Flu?

Since it is obvious that hostility has permeated society, the question we need to ask is, "How can it be changed?"

Those who examine organizational structures conclude that in the vast majority of cases the leader determines the culture. That's who sets the moral tone, establishes the rules, forms the structures, and controls the decision-making process. Teamwork and cooperation is not a "bottoms up" operation. The impetus for harmony in the orchestra starts with the conductor.

A friend who works at an accounting firm told me, "I've noticed that when my boss comes to work unhappy about something, the entire department gets the blues."

It's not only true at work, but at home.

A recent study reported in the *Journal of Marriage and the Family* concludes that exposure to negative emotions can give you emotional flu. It's like a chain reaction that moves through a family—and has the same effect on a team or an organization.

David Almedia of the University of Arizona was involved in the research. He states, "This work brings new awareness that being in a negative mood, being unaccessible or generally grouchy, can have a noxious effect on the well-being of our families."[2]

The study discovered these alarming facts:

1. Bad feelings tend to be more potent and have longer-lasting effects than positive emotions.
2. Fathers bringing home negative vibes from work that affect other family members are a common pattern.
3. Emotions are most often passed from husband to wife and from parents to children.

Almedia concluded, "We know from long study that distressed parents tend to have distressed children."

Since attitudes are highly contagious, leaders need to avoid spreading germs of gloom and turn to positive prescriptions.

The Problem Solver

If you were hired to lead the turnaround of an organization where strife, discord, and hostility reigned supreme, what actions would you take? Here are seven steps to follow:

1. Start with an open mind, not an agenda. You may know exactly what is necessary for a quick resolution, but hold your fire. Follow this basic rule: Questions always come before answers. That's why you should spend several weeks in one-on-one conversations and small-group meetings asking hundreds of questions.

Become a sponge rather than a faucet. There's a time and place for your ideas to flow. However, early in the process is not the time. You are there to listen—and to absorb everything you hear.

2. Believe in the honesty and decency of people. Build trust by expressing your heartfelt faith in both the goodness and the potential of your associates. If that belief isn't present, you may not be the right person for the task. You can't transfer confidence and expectation unless it is genuine.

Now express your belief. You'll never know what it means to a staff member when you pat that person on the shoulder and say, "I'm really glad you're part of this team."

In Florida I had a long conversation with a friend who talked about his father—who had recently passed away. "It was my dad's total faith in me that kept me on the straight and narrow. I could never do anything to let him down."

3. Don't avoid uncomfortable topics. The mark of an effective leader is the ability to confront troublesome issues head-on. Why? Rumors and hearsay expand in a vacuum—and can explode like a volcano. Avoidance only heightens the predicament.

When a medical clinic in South Carolina was having a severe cash-flow problem, the administrator immediately called the entire staff together—doctors, lab technicians, secretaries, and maintenance workers—to explain the problem in detail. Instead of panic, the meeting produced a bonding that helped the clinic weather the storm.

4. Deal with issues, not personalities. Don't allow a conflict to become personal. Even if the discord does involve the behavior of an individual, never resort to name-calling. Instead, take the high road and frame the discussion around policies and procedures. It's the integrity of the organization that is at stake.

Kenneth Cloke, director of the Center for Dispute Resolution, says, "Be hard on the problem and soft on the people. Shift the focus of the conflict from personalities and people to problem solving and organizational growth."[3]

5. Maintain a consistent leadership style. "I never know where she's coming from," complained a teacher in a suburban Philadelphia elementary school about her principal. "One day she's full of honey, and the next day she's heartless."

Riding a roller coaster may seem like fun at an amusement park, but sudden ups and downs don't produce a healthy environment for work. If your goal is to reduce tension and resolve conflict, be sure your leadership style is both positive and consistent. Make sure your reputation can be described with words such as *compassionate*, *encouraging*, and *caring*.

6. Create social time with your associates. After a speaking engagement at a conference in Oklahoma, I slipped into a workshop on the topic "Friendships in the Workplace." The discussion centered on whether a leader should have close friends within the organization—or limit socializing to outside acquaintances.

The consensus was that special relationships with associates produce jealousy in the staff and can make it difficult for the leader to be even-handed in enforcing rules and regulations.

A wiser path is to meet frequently with small groups of team members. For example, a computer software firm in Palo Alto, California, formed a "Nine-Hole Golf League" where executives and employees played together every Tuesday evening during the summer.

7. *Always follow the affirmative path.* In the decision-making process it's advantageous to make lists of the "pros" and "cons" of an issue before choosing. Use a similar technique for resolving internal conflict. Try creating a road map that leads to a solution. Along the path mark the side roads and detours and list the dangers. When the time comes to make the journey, follow only the affirmative trail.

How Big Is the Problem?

Don't fall into the trap of seeing conflicts larger than they really are.

I heard about a farmer in Missouri who fretted for years over a huge rock—at least fifteen feet across—in the middle of his field. Many times he had broken plowshares and other pieces of equipment when he hit that outcropping. Every time the farmer came near it he grumbled and complained. "I hate that rock," he told his neighbors.

Finally, he decided to remove that giant stone—no matter how large it was. He borrowed some heavy equipment and was ready to dig as deep as necessary. He planned to surround it with giant cables and excavate it from his property.

"I must have started on the wrong side," he said after digging with a shovel and finding the rock only twelve inches thick. It was the same on the other side—only a foot thick. With a crowbar he was able to move the long, thin stone. He broke it apart and easily hauled the pieces away. Is there something in your life that has been bothering you for years? Perhaps it is much smaller than you think.

A Smooth Scolding

As sure as the sun will rise tomorrow there will be times when you need to offer correction—whether you are dealing with your own children or those you supervise at work. Here are four "Principles of Criticism" to practice:

1. **Never point out errors without offering a solution.**
   One of the greatest frustrations of subordinates is "they always tell me what is wrong, but never suggest how to make it right." The time for correction must also become a time to teach.

2. **Criticize the act, never the person.**
   Instead of saying, "John, will you ever learn to add?" say, "John, I think you'd better recheck those numbers." Why deflate someone's ego when your goal is to improve performance? People have emotions that need to be respected.

3. **Never scold in public.**
   Even if the error is minor, don't embarrass someone by pointing out mistakes in front of colleagues. And, when possible, have the chat where the person is most comfortable—rather than saying, "I need to see you in my office."

4. Always end with praise.
Some people believe you should start with a compliment and end with correction. I reverse it—preferring to end on a positive note.

Laugh at Your Critics

Any good automobile mechanic will tell you that your engine will be at peak performance when every spark plug, piston, and valve is in perfect working condition. Just one defective part can cause havoc. If you are not careful, the same will be true about the people you associate with.

You may ask, "What should I do about someone who is constantly telling me why I will fail, or is criticizing every decision I make?" Perhaps that person is very close to you—a family member or a lifelong friend. It is important to use diplomacy in dealing with toxic people.

You should not make a rash decision to suddenly disassociate yourself from individuals who are stumbling blocks to your future. See these people for what they truly are and learn to appreciate both their strengths and weaknesses. You will finally learn how to enjoy their company, while brushing off their critical advice.

You'll find a great sense of empowerment when you learn how to love the best parts of someone's personality and laugh at their shortcomings.

Needed: Toxic Handlers

Research by Peter Frost and Sandra Robinson at the University of British Columbia found that there are a growing number of people in business whose major responsibility is to "manage organizational pain" and to remove "mental toxins" in the workplace.[4]

Who has the responsibility of reducing conflict and tension in an organization? Senior managers who deal with troubled colleagues.

Here are the five major traits of a toxic handler.

1. They are great listeners.
2. They can be trusted with a confidence.
3. They sense when trouble is brewing and act behind the scenes before it erupts.
4. They reframe difficult messages into instructions that can be implemented.
5. They identify and activate solutions.

You may not have the title of "toxic handler," but you can certainly achieve great results by designating yourself to be a peacemaker in your work environment. Why not give it a try?

Regardless of how stress-filled the atmosphere may be, the tensions can be reduced.

One of the most confrontational spots on earth is the line of demarcation between North and South Korea. Soldiers warily eye each other across a border laden with countless land mines and surrounded by heavy artillery. It's been called "the last Cold War frontier."

Yet recently at Panmunjom, which straddles the tense border, a Czech pianist played a sonata from Beethoven's "The Storm" and other selections. The concert, organized by Swedish, Swiss, and Polish delegations, was the first such recital in the heavily fortified frontier zone dividing the two Koreas. Both sides were watching and listening.

"We believe bringing culture to this place of confrontation and tension is a way of confidence building," said Swedish Major General Sven Julin. "We hope this [concert] may contribute to gradually changing the frosty atmosphere still prevailing here."[5]

If soothing music can help bring calm to a troubled war zone, why not use a little Beethoven to add some peace and tranquility to your own life?

REMINDERS FOR LEADERS WHO LOVE

- Negative emotions create a chain reaction.
- Have an open mind, not an agenda.
- Believe in the honesty and decency of people.
- Don't avoid unpleasant topics.
- Deal with issues, not personalities.
- Maintain a consistent leadership style.
- Create social time with your associates.
- Always follow the affirmative path.
- Become a "toxic handler."

Conflict is a symptom, not the cause. The seeds you plant by transforming the culture can produce a more tranquil and satisfying world.

13

Building Shatterproof Relationships

■ The number one reason for failure and unhappiness—both at home and in society—is the inability to get along with others. According to one study, "more than 95 percent of men and women let go from their jobs over a ten-year period were fired because of poor social skills rather than lack of competence or technical ability."[1]

Our interaction with others is the glue that holds people and institutions together. Without it there is loneliness, self-pity, and boredom. Edward Hallowell, M.D., a senior lecturer at Harvard Medical School, says, "To thrive, indeed just to survive, we need warmhearted contact with other people. The close-to-the-vest, standoffish life is bad for your body and your soul. Like a vitamin deficiency, a human contact deficiency weakens the body, the mind, and the spirit."[2]

How powerful are relationships? They can mark the difference between life and death. Dr. Lisa Berkman of the Harvard School of Public Health headed a study that followed the lives of seven thousand people in Alameda County, California, for nine years. They inquired whether the people were married or lived alone, what kind of contact they had with friends and relatives, and whether or not they belonged to a church or other religious organizations.

When they evaluated the group's risk of dying, "the most isolated people were three times more likely to die in that nine-year period than those with stronger social ties."[3]

What lesson can we learn? Plug into the lives of others and build relationships that last.

Ten Valuable Keys

Personal alliances don't just materialize out of thin air. Certainly there are times when you "click" with someone, but most relationships are established much like a farmer grows a crop. The ground is cultivated, seeds are planted, and there is plenty of watering and nurturing before the harvest.

To build bonds of friendship that will stand the test of time, here are ten important keys:

Key #1: Realize that strong relationships are primary.

Your biographical sketch may tell the world about your education, your expertise, and the positions you have held, yet your most important attribute is probably hidden. How do you get along with others?

In their book *The Healing Manager,* William and Kathleen Lundin state, "Relationships are Job One. Product quality and efficiency experts come second. Corporate leaders have to stop denying the existence of emotions at work."[4]

Here are the priorities they establish: "Relationship, then quality. Values, then efficiency. Beliefs, then cooperation. Caring, then loyalty. Personal growth, then success."

Studies have demonstrated the fact that more than 80 percent of all sales are based on the customer liking the salesperson.

Tom Watson Jr., who built IBM into an international powerhouse, stated that his most important contribution to the corporation was his ability to "pick strong and intelligent men and then hold them together by persuasion, by apologies, by financial incentives, by speeches, by chatting with their wives, by thoughtfulness when they were sick or involved in accidents, and using every tool at my command to make that team think that I was a decent guy."[5]

Key #2: Learn to truly "understand" others.

Here is a question I've used a hundred times when meeting people in their place of employment: "How did you ever get into a job like this?"

The frequent reply is, "Do you really want to know?" Or, "Do you have two hours?"

Well, since I asked the question, they usually don't hesitate to begin telling me their life history—and that's exactly what I wanted.

You will never begin to understand someone unless you take the time to listen to their personal story. To me, it's always fascinating, never boring.

Philip Crosby, who has been called "the leader of America's quality revolution," states that people relate to those who they feel understand them. He said that during his military career in two wars, "all my time was spent in the enlisted ranks. We had our own rules, and we responded to those officers who responded to us. We made some of them very successful, and we let others fall to their natural level. Some of our leaders pretended to relate and some actually did. We could always tell the difference. It is not possible to fool the people for very long."[6]

Key #3: Relationships begin at home.

"Why doesn't Dad have time to play with me at night?" a five-year-old asked his mother before bedtime.

The mom replied, "He's been promoted and that means more work, honey."

"Well, why don't they put him in a slower group?" said the boy.

We may smile at the youngster's response, but the problem is deadly serious. In their misguided attempt to climb the ladder called success, far too many people ignore the foundation of all relationships—their own family. Somehow they have concluded that it is more important to socialize with colleagues than to spend time with those who count the most.

In recent research at Harvard's Graduate School of Education, sixty-five families were followed over an eight-year period to determine which family activities were of more value to child development, comparing such activities as playtime, school time, and family dinnertime. Dinnertime was the winner.

If there are children in your home, make it a habit that during the evening meal they are expected to discuss a current event which *they* bring to the table, not you.

When strong bonds are a priority at home, alliances in the community, at church, and on the job will flow naturally.

Key #4: Build relationships based on principles.

We are driven by our core beliefs and guided by our moral compass.

The president of a small midwestern college told me, "Every fall, during freshmen orientation week, I stand in the cafeteria and observe as students are making new friends. Leaders gravitate toward leaders and trouble-makers are pulled to those of their kind." Then he added, "It's as if a magnet draws certain types of people to each other."

Since the "like attract like" principle is at work, make certain that your standards are high and your ethics are beyond dispute. As a leader, do whatever it takes to ensure that those you surround yourself with have the same ideals. Then treat those people with the honor and respect they deserve.

The "Golden Rule" is not just a platitude or a cliché. It is a fixed law of God. Jesus stated, "So in everything, do to others what you would have them do to you" (Matt. 7:12). And he declared, "A new command I give you: Love one another. As I have loved you, so you must love one another" (John 13:34).

Key #5: Set an example that backs up your words.

A large defense plant in Maryland needed an assistant to the chief accountant. The advertisement read: "This is not an executive position; therefore, it necessitates con-siderable work."

Some people have the opinion that if they could only move into the ranks of leadership they'd have a cushy job. Far from it. Those who take responsibility seriously understand the weight and burden it brings.

Who is a real leader? It is one who:

- Stops to pick up a gum wrapper on the hallway floor.
- Says, "Let me help you," in an emergency.
- Never sidesteps an agreed-upon policy.

Instead of saying, "Let me tell you how to do it," say, "Allow me to show you how it's done."

If every team member mirrored your behavior, what kind of an organization would yours be?

Key #6: Create an "open door" environment.

In Missouri I spoke at a workshop for guidance counselors that was held in a large church. After the session I was invited by the senior minister to take a tour of the facility. The final stop was his office—a spacious room with a large window between him and the outer office where his secretary worked.

"I notice you don't have shades or blinds on the window," I commented. "Aren't there times when you need some privacy?"

He laughed. "Privacy? I learned a long time ago that when you stay in full view of people you can't be accused of anything. I not only keep an open-door policy, but an open-window policy too."

The leader who creates a cloistered, secluded office in a distant corner of the building sends a signal that says, "Don't bother me. I want to be left alone." Those in the organization conclude that such a person is detached, aloof, and unapproachable.

To avoid such an image, many successful managers have relocated their office to the center of activity—often without the typical trappings of an executive suite. And they are sincere when they say, "My door is always open."

Key #7: Demonstrate personal and professional courtesy.

As a young man, I was introduced to Dr. George Crane, a Chicago psychologist who for years wrote a popular syndicated newspaper column. What I still remember about the conversation was his advice to join the "Compliment Club."

Dr. Crane said, "Every day I deliberately pay a sincere compliment to at least three people." He gave these examples: "Yesterday I bragged on a young mother for the way she dressed her child. I told a grocery store clerk I liked the way he smiled. And I congratulated a bank manager on how tidy he kept his desk."

That simple idea made an indelible impression on me. The next day I began looking for reasons to applaud or praise—and I found plenty. Today, many years later, I no longer think about the "Compliment Club." It is an automatic daily habit.

In my experience, people I consider extraordinary are those who take the time to show personal concern and demonstrate courtesy. They ask, "How is your wife and son?" They send "Thank you" notes and offer sincere compliments.

Key #8: Realize that change requires connection.

Why have you been placed in charge? Someone expects you to move an organization or a concept to a higher level. You are seen as a *change agent*.

The secret of dynamic transformation is not power, authority, and control. Rather, it is found in relationships. Permanent, effective change is the result of being connected. I like the observation of Reg Jones, the former head of General Electric. He said, "The CEO finds it much easier to work, as a carpenter would say, with the grain rather than across the grain. You can change a corporate culture but you do it largely by working with that culture, and not counter to it."[7]

You may have a lofty vision and a flawless master plan, yet your most ambitious dream will fail without creating a team that will make it happen. Before revealing your concepts and ideas, spend as long as it takes to:

- Develop a personal rapport with every person you will be working with.
- Determine the goals and objectives of your associates.
- Create an environment for the free flow of ideas.
- Share small parts of your proposal until others take ownership and say, "Yes. I'd like to give that a try!"
- Give team members credit for transformation and change.

Key #9: Never betray a confidence.

I was once asked, "What is the number one way to build a friendship—and to keep a friend?"

The answer is uncomplicated. "Learn to keep a secret," I replied.

At a recent luncheon with friends, the topic surfaced about someone who had left his job on short notice. The person who knew the details was asked, "Well, what did he say was the reason?"

"I'm sorry, I cannot say, because it was told to me in strict confidence," he replied.

The topic quickly changed, but I thought about that conversation later. If I ever needed someone to talk with, where would I turn? I would gravitate toward the person I knew I could trust. In fact, my opinion of this man's character grew immensely when he spoke that one sentence about confidentiality.

Since friendships are built on faith, you are going to be given the "trust" test. Someone will say, "If I share this with you, will you promise not to tell anyone?"

Don't glibly respond "Yes." Your integrity is about to be challenged. The moment someone shares a private matter with you, vow to yourself that the information will not leave your lips.

Realize also that keeping a confidence is a two-way street. Can you be certain that the intimate facts you divulge will stay private? In the words of a Spanish proverb, "To whom you tell your secrets, to him you resign your liberty."

Key #10: Stay connected—no matter what!

Relationships are active, not passive. To be effective they must be seen as a work in progress.

The owner of a small video-production firm recently told me about an argument he had with a former employee. "I really flew off the handle and chewed the fellow out. He left in a huff and never came back."

Why was he telling me the story? Today that same former worker is the vice president of a large firm the owner would love to have as a client. "I learned my lesson," he told me. "The bridge you burn is one you may need to walk across someday."

Value and nurture every association—even if you become separated by time or space. If you spend weeks, months, and years developing an alliance, don't let it die. Pick up the phone, send a fax, write an e-mail, stay in touch!

From Your Heart

Centuries ago there was a poor artist who was a guest for a summer in a beautiful castle. When it came time to leave he realized that he had nothing to give his hosts for their hospitality.

Before he left, he shut himself in his room for several days with the door locked. When he finally departed, a servant found the sheets of his bed missing. Were they stolen? No!

The sheets were discovered by the family, neatly rolled in the corner of the room. When they were unrolled there was a spectacular picture of Alexander in the tent of Darius painted on them.

The guest's most valuable asset was not his artistic ability. It was his humble attitude. He had a desire to leave the best possible gift. And he gave it without saying a word.

A true relationship is a matter of the heart. Let your actions create bonds that can never be broken.

REMINDERS FOR LEADERS WHO LOVE

- Realize that strong relationships are primary.
- Learn to truly "understand" others.
- Relationships begin at home.

- Build alliances based on principles.
- Set an example that backs up your words.
- Create an "open door" environment.
- Demonstrate personal and professional courtesy.
- Realize that change requires connection.
- Never betray a confidence.
- Stay connected—no matter what!

Relationships grow strong when you inspire, encourage, brighten, and cheer. In the words of Albert Schweitzer, "The true worth of man is not to be found in man himself, but in the colors and texture that come alive in others."[8]

14

Communicating from the Inside Out

■ In the pediatrics section of a major hospital, infants needing special care were dying at a much higher rate than expected. The medical staff searched for the cause—faulty procedures, infections, and other theories. Finally, an elderly volunteer said, "I think I know why those babies are dying. You have separated these infants from their mothers, who need to love, cuddle, and talk to them."

Immediately they instituted a program where the babies were held while they ate, snuggled after their diapers were changed, and even sung to by the volunteers. Almost instantly the mortality rate dropped.

Emotional attachment is not only necessary for children, it is essential in every arena of life. Why do so many brilliant, talented people fail to rise to their potential? They haven't learned how to communicate from the heart.

How's Your EI?

For decades, people have believed, "To get ahead all you have to do is be smart and work hard." They are wrong! Current research tells us that intelligence (your IQ) accounts for only between 4 percent and 15 percent of an individual's job success. There is something that is twice as important—your Emotional Intelligence.

In his book *Working with Emotional Intelligence*, Daniel Goleman, former science editor at *The New York Times*, says, "The rules for work are changing. We're being judged by a new yardstick; not just by how smart we are, or by our training and expertise, but also how well we handle ourselves and each other."[1]

What are the EI competencies? On the personal side they include self-awareness, self-regulation, and motivation. Socially, they include empathy, skills for communicating, and inducing desirable responses in others.

Six Goals

I'm sure you have heard someone say, "When you get to know her, she is really a nice person." Or, "Don't be fooled by first impressions. He's not as mean as he sounds."

Let's hope your friends don't need to make those excuses for you!

Stop for a moment and ask yourself these questions:

"What image do I project to people who meet me for the first time?"

"Do I deliberately create barriers between me and my associates?"

"Do I come across as being shrill, aggressive, pushy, or arrogant?"

I'm not suggesting that someone can change his or her persona overnight, but there are workable strategies you can adopt that your associates will welcome. Here are six objectives worth pursuing:

1. *Express your heartfelt feelings.* When a small town in Texas was looking for a new city manager, several department heads were asked, "What's the most important quality of the person we should be seeking?"

One woman summed up the feelings of the group when she said, "It should be a person who can be believed."

The most effective way for any individual to overcome imperfections and weaknesses is through transparency—by expressing and displaying true feelings. Since most people can "see through" a facade, it's futile to try to be something you are not. As author Denis Waitley says, "The tongue can lie, but the body acts instinctively, subconsciously, and honestly." And he adds, "People telegraph their intentions and feelings without ever realizing what is happening."[2]

It's important to realize that the words you utter are more than ideas created in your mind. The Bible says, "Out of the abundance of the heart the mouth speaketh" (Matt. 12:34 KJV).

2. *Become a passionate communicator.* Before every important meeting, take the time to reflect on what you believe. Then, when the moment is right, share your convictions with zeal and passion. Let people know your deep feelings on the topic.

There's a great gulf, however, between being compassionate and being aggressive. Avoid any tendency to appear inflexible or domineering on the issue.

Connie Podesta, an executive trainer, says, "Aggressive communicators may meet their short-term needs and goals, but they will not create or strengthen the kind of relationships that can accommodate open communication. What they fail to realize is that a relationship based on guilt, fear and control can never be successful or healthy in the long run."[3]

Whether you are engaged in a one-on-one conversation or standing before a large audience, let people know what you are feeling on the inside. Allow your words to *reflect* those sentiments. Nido Quebein, a noted public speaker, offers this advice, "If something is wonderful, say it like it's wonderful; if something is sad, say it like it's sad; if something is important, say it like it's important."[4]

3. Don't be known as a critic. Before each major political race, almost every candidate running for office publicly vows, "I will not engage in any personal attacks on my opponent."

Then, as the campaign gets hotter than a boiling kettle, the pledge is somehow moved to the back burner. The candidate will say, "I wasn't talking about John personally, I was attacking him on the issues."

Great leaders win on vision, inspiration, and positive ideas—not on denigrating others. As Donald Krause said in his book *The Way of the Leader,* "One notable characteristic of an effective leader is that he does not have time to criticize other people. Never tell people how to do things. Tell them your objectives and they will surprise you with their ingenuity."[5]

Your image and reputation is constantly being shaped. Decide today that if you can't find something positive to say about an individual, you will choose silence. As one of my college professors said, "Once the toothpaste is out of the tube, it's hard to get it back in."

Instead of talking about people, steer the conversation toward important ideas.

4. Avoid gossip and idle chatter. You'll never be able to eliminate busybodies who love to spread the latest rumor on the grapevine. So instead of being harmed by the process, learn to make it work on your behalf. Here are ways to make that happen:

- Brag about your boss behind his back. Before the day is over, someone will say, "You'll never believe what (your name) says about you!"
- Never pass on a negative rumor. You don't want your name to be associated with harmful gossip.
- Avoid uttering a phrase you don't want attributed to you.
- Don't become defensive when someone says something negative about you. Counter it by a friendly conversation with the "source," and calmly tell others the truth.

Also remember that a vacuum is created when you fail to communicate—and that empty space will be filled with idle hearsay and misrepresentation. That's why you need to keep positive information flowing.

5. Leave a paper trail. A friend who worked in the White House during the George Bush administration in the late 1980s showed me a scrapbook of notes the president had written to him. Bush was a master at personal communication—and he established a great bond with his team members as a result.

Placing your thoughts on paper yields two valuable results: (1) clearer communications and (2) stronger relationships.

I like what author Harvey MacKay says: "If the house is on fire, forget the china, silver and wedding album—grab the Rolodex."[6]

6. Monitor your attitude. It has long been known that it takes the average mind up to 50 percent longer to understand and digest a negative statement than a positive one. That's why it is just as important to speak positively as to think positively.

One of the bright lights on the professional speaking circuit is Keith Harrell, who is addressing corporate executives worldwide on the topic "Attitude Is Everything."

Keith, who is six-foot-six, was captain of his basketball team at Seattle University, but he wasn't drafted into the NBA. However, people constantly come up to him and ask, "You play with the NBA?" He smiles and answers, "Yes, I do. I play with my Natural Born Abilities, and I'm slam dunking every day!"[7]

Keith got a taste for speaking as an employee at IBM. He was asked to introduce a new computer model at a regional marketing and sales force meeting. Knowing how dry those events could be, Keith decided to inject his own personality into the presentation and made it more like a revival meeting than a data-filled speech. People left the room saying, "I believe! I believe!"

We all need to adopt the philosophy Keith espouses: "The only difference between a bad day and a good day is attitude."

It is also important to incorporate the habit of ending every conversation with a note of optimism about the future. Use phrases such as:

"I'm really excited about this project."

"I believe this is going to produce great things."

"I am looking forward to working with you."

When you exude enthusiasm and confidence about tomorrow, a growing number of people will request the pleasure of your company.

Friendly Persuasion

If your goal is to produce positive change, make certain you communicate from your heart. For example, here are the rules to follow if you want to convince others to adopt a new position:

- Don't place people on the defensive. If you tell them, "I'm going to change your mind"—they'll dig in their heels and challenge you, rather than agree.
- Never insult your opponent. Even if you hint that your adversary is ignorant, or ill-informed, you create an enemy rather than a future partner.
- Talk in terms of what the other person wants, not what you desire.
- Thoroughly know your listeners' opinions, beliefs, and attitudes. Start from where "they" are, not from your position.
- Begin with what you agree upon, not your differences.
- Articulate both sides of the argument. Let people know you are knowledgeable of the opposing position.
- Never lose your cool—or display your anger.
- Stick with the facts. Don't stretch the truth or embellish the details.
- Ask for their agreement kindly and sincerely—but don't fail to ask.

The key to change is to touch someone's heart and build on what you have in common. Burt Nanus, professor of management at the University of Southern California, says, "The head and the heart are connected, of course, and failure of either leads to quick demise. Even skillful visionary leadership will fail if there is no shared sense of purpose or empowerment to act."[8]

REMINDERS FOR LEADERS WHO LOVE

- "Emotional intelligence" is necessary for success.
- Express your heartfelt feelings.
- Become a passionate communicator.
- Don't be known as a critic.
- Avoid gossip and idle chatter.
- Leave a paper trail.
- Monitor your attitude.
- Emphasize what you have in common.

Why is it vital that your heart is clean and pure? Communication never ceases. Even when silence reigns, your presence is sending messages loud and clear—speaking from the inside out!

15

The Power and Might of Mercy

■ The story of Fanny Crosby contains a great lesson of life.

Just six weeks after she was born (in New York state, 1820) the child developed a minor eye inflammation. Because of a country doctor's improper medical treatment Fanny became permanently blind.

Her lack of sight proved to be no handicap. Fanny Crosby became known as the "Hymn Queen"—writing over eight thousand hymns before she died at the age of ninety-five.

Fanny, who wrote "Blessed Assurance" and so many popular hymns, felt it was her lack of vision that allowed her to create the melodies and poems.

Did she harbor any bitterness against the physician? No. She forgave him and once said, "If I could meet the doctor now, I would thank him over and over again for making me blind." Fanny believed her impairment was a gift.

What path do you choose when misfortune and adversity suddenly strike? Is it the road of accusation, condemnation, and blame? Or have you discovered the power of forgiveness, compassion, and mercy?

Your friends don't expect you to be a flawless diamond. Far from it. They know that under the scrutiny of a microscope we all have blemishes and imperfections. What they do expect is that you will readily acknowledge your errors. As business consultant Lester Bittel observes, "Subordinates like to know their bosses are right most of the time. But there is also something endearing about a boss who can make a mistake and admit it. Such leaders are likely to be especially popular if they can forgive the mistakes of their employees."[1]

"Seventy Times Seven"

One of the first lessons of "Love Leadership 101" is learning to say, "Will you forgive me?"

There are many who never truly "bury the hatchet." Instead they build a memorial to the incident and brag about it again and again. Remember, "I can forgive, but I cannot forget," is only another way of saying, "I cannot forgive."

Peter asked Jesus, "How many times shall I forgive my brother when he sins against me? Up to seven times?" (Matt. 18:21). "Not seven times," Jesus replied, "but seventy-seven times!" (v. 22).

If you ever see two men with clenched fists, one thing is certain: it is impossible for them to shake hands. They need to relax and demonstrate forgiveness—what Josh McDowell calls the "oil of relationships."

Some people only forgive after they "get even" with their enemy, yet that only increases the conflict. The Bible tells us, "The discretion of a man makes him slow to anger, and his glory is to overlook a transgression" (Prov. 19:11 NKJV).

Most leadership skills are the result of knowledge, action, and repetition. However, mercy is not a learned craft or technique. It is the outcome of a covenant and commitment made deep within your heart and soul. It is all-encompassing. As British theologian Donald Guthrie observes, "The root meaning of 'mercy' is compassion, hence it is closely linked with love."[2]

A refreshing development has been the openness of many in government, business, and the arts to share their spiritual values. For example, media pundits didn't quite know how to respond when George W. Bush was asked, "Whom do you consider the greatest philosopher?" His answer: "Jesus Christ. Because He changed my life."

Should Leaders Cry?

How do people react when faced with a predicament that seems too tough to handle? Many are like Linus in the "Peanuts" comic strip. One day he said to Charlie Brown, "There's no problem too big we can't run away from."

Others may put on a brave front and, without emotion, attempt to confront the challenge. True achievers, however, don't listen to the old adage "real leaders don't cry." Often, their tears are a sign of their strength.

I have never known a crisis that dealt only with physical property or "things." Whether it is an earthquake or a business failure, the ultimate tragedy is always measured in human terms. Lives are torn apart, emotions are on edge, and true leaders will find their shoulders damp with tears.

I believe one of the reasons women have made such great strides in leadership is because they have a natural tendency to be sensitive and nurturing. Failure comes when they attempt to mimic role models who are aggressive and confrontational.

Your River of Life

Mercy can be measured by what we give to others—emotionally, physically, and sometimes financially.

On a journey to Israel I visited the Sea of Galilee—a fresh lake that is brimming with life. It is alive because it gives out a portion of all it receives, flowing into the river Jordan.

At the south end of the Jordan is the Dead Sea, the saltiest body of water in the world. It bears that name because there is no outlet; it keeps all it receives and can sustain no animal life.

The lesson is clear. Giving keeps us dynamic and alive.

It's been said that we are not cisterns made for hoarding—we are channels made for sharing. You were born with two hands, *one to receive and the other to give.*

More Than Trinkets

In Ohio I met an automobile salesman who had an incredible track record—selling to many of the same families for three generations. "What is your secret?" I asked. "Why do you have so many repeat customers?"

"Early in my career I decided to make friends by giving things away," he told me. "Every morning, before leaving home, I made sure my pockets were filled with little trinkets—from ballpoint pens with the company logo to wrapped candy and key chains. I tried to give something to every customer."

He told me that while the parents were looking at the car, he would give their child a coin to put in the gumball machine. "I made it a point to give something to everybody."

Why did it work? People never forget those who are thoughtful and generous.

While you shouldn't give for the purpose of receiving, that is the way it usually seems to turn out. A generous donor was once asked, "How do you manage to give so much?" He responded, "The good Lord never stops shoveling good things on me. If I didn't shovel it back, I'd be buried in an avalanche!"

It's been said that there are two kinds of people, givers and takers. The takers eat well, but the givers sleep well!

Touching Lives

Throughout Great Britain, the day after Christmas is also celebrated. It's called "Boxing Day."

In the Middle Ages, the lords and ladies of England presented Christmas gifts in boxes to the servants on this day and a tradition was established. Boxes of food were often distributed. It was also the time the "alms boxes" of donations given during the holiday season were opened in the churches and their contents shared with the poor of the parish.

Boxing Day, also known as St. Stephen's Day, is still celebrated in the United Kingdom, Australia, New Zealand, and Canada. Many people give gifts on this day to employees and special people such as those who deliver the paper or the mail.

There are many who touch our lives that merit recognition. However, don't wait for a holiday to express your thanks—anytime is the right time for gratitude.

Take This Job!

Frequently we focus on forgiving others when the problem is with ourselves. For example, when a man or woman despises their work, it is often not the job or the associates, it's the person.

Why do I say that? I have watched people move from company to company and city to city, yet within a short time they are unhappy again with their circumstances. In other words, they are carrying their troubles with them.

If you want to start loving your work, here are six suggestions:

1. Step back a few paces from the problem and view it as an outsider. Say, "Now isn't that interesting!"
2. Write down exactly what is bothering you about the situation and talk it out with a trusted friend.
3. Start smiling. That's right—walk around with a pleasant look, even in the midst of chaos.
4. Every day, when you arrive at work, make it your mission to change the situation rather than be upset by it.
5. Look for emotional fulfillment from your family, friends, recreation, and church—rather than from your job.
6. Forgive yourself for the way you have viewed your work, your associates, and your career.

A Turning Point

The real test of mercy in the marketplace occurs when you find it necessary to dismiss a long-term employee. Once, when an organization was downsizing, I was given the unpleasant task of calling in several people—one by one—to tell them the firm could no longer afford to keep them on the payroll.

I wanted to repeat what my dad told me when he disciplined me as a child: "This hurts me more than it hurts you!"

Instead, I looked at the firings as an opportunity to move people from a moment of despair to seeing the event as a major turning point. "Someday you will look back on this time and realize how important it was for your future," I would say. "In fact, when we meet again one or two years from now, you will probably tell me you are *glad* this happened."

Throughout the process, I did my best to assure these people that our friendship was more important than the decision of an organization—and I meant it when I said, "I want to help you find the right position as soon as possible. Call me as often as you need to."

Why is leading with love and mercy vital? It is your warmth that will someday help to soften a harsh decision you may have to make.

Reminders for Leaders Who Love

- Be quick to acknowledge your errors.
- Forgiveness is the outgrowth of a personal commitment.
- Tears are a sign of strength.
- Mercy can be measured by our giving.
- We are channels made for sharing.
- Anytime is the right time for gratitude.

- Before forgiving others we must forgive ourselves.
- Mercy softens the hard decisions of life.

We may be able to herd sheep and drive cattle, but those methods eventually backfire with people. In the short run there may be progress attributed to force or intimidation, but it will never last. The only leadership that prevails is based on love, mercy, and mutual respect.

16

Love That Leads Forever

■ I felt extremely fortunate when a friend called and asked, "Would you be interested in going to the Masters Golf Tournament next week?"

Without hesitating, I exclaimed, "Yes!"

Tickets to the annual Georgia event had been in the man's family since the 1950s.

The azaleas were in full bloom, the course was the most beautiful I've ever seen, and it was a thrill to watch Tiger Woods hit some incredible drives. The memory that will probably linger with me longest, however, is what I saw during the annual par-three tournament, the day before the Masters began.

I claimed a spot just behind the golfers as they teed off on hole number three. It's a downhill ninety-yard shot to a green on the edge of a lake. I watched Greg Norman, Arnold Palmer, Ben Crenshaw, and other golfing greats hit some delicate shots. Then came a man I didn't recognize from watching the pros on television.

"Who's that?" I asked an Augusta National official dressed in a green jacket. "Oh, that's Paul Runyan. They invite former champions to play in this event, and he won the PGA in 1934 and 1938."

I watched, fascinated, as this ninety-one-year-old golfer hit a master stroke that landed close to the pin. And when Runyan made birdie on the hole, the crowd gave him the greatest ovation of the day.

"Now there's a man who really loves this sport," the fellow next to me said.

Respect, Honor, and Commitment

On Sunday, as my wife and I watched Vijay Singh, from Fiji, win the green jacket with his precision game, I was again struck by the devotion golf fans have given to this particular event. There is a feeling that Augusta National is hallowed ground. Not once did I witness boisterous behavior or notice trash carelessly discarded on the ground. People, showing reverence, spoke only in hushed whispers.

There was absolutely no commercialization—no booths promoting corporations or flyers with ads of sponsors. And there was no price gouging. Sandwiches were $1.75 and soft drinks were $1.00. A ticket for the entire four-day tournament is $100, and they could easily charge $1,000 or more. The patron list was closed in 1972 and the waiting list halted six years later.

What does it take to become the best? Follow Augusta National's example. Respect your mission, honor the people you serve, and commit yourself to a love that will last forever.

Time to Rejoice!

I asked my friend George Harland to reflect on his years as an executive with the Cadillac division of General Motors. "It certainly wasn't about cars," he said, "it was about the people."

Once, when Harland was running the company's operation in Chicago, he received a phone call from his superiors in Detroit. "George, you've exceeded the sales targets for this year and we're anxious for you to come to headquarters so we can honor you."

"No," replied George. "I'd like you to fly to Chicago and thank the people who made it happen. I'm not the one who should be lauded."

A few weeks later, at a lavish catered banquet, Harland's team was applauded by the top brass from Cadillac. "It was a night they will never forget," Harland said.

When love-based leadership produces a victory, look for every opportunity to honor and cheer.

- The admissions office of a Pennsylvania college throws a party if they reach their enrollment goals.
- A product development company in Arizona has a celebration every time they are granted a new patent.
- A petroleum firm in Houston strikes up the band when they uncover a new oil field.

The rejoicing is not for the organization but for the people who have made something exciting happen. When leaders love those they serve, it shows.

What Makes the Difference?

In this book we have focused on how genuine affection for those around you enhances your leadership capabilities, yet there is something more. It also affects the bottom line.

I have met scores of people who are either in top management or who have accumulated a substantial amount of money—and they have similar traits. It's their personality, drive, and people skills—rarely their training or education—that makes the difference.

Thomas Stanley, author of *The Millionaire Mind,* interviewed over 1,200 millionaires and discovered some fascinating results. For example, the average person in the study made Bs and Cs in college—and the average SAT score was between 1100 and 1190, not good enough to get into many of the top universities.

Most people believe that to become financially successful you need a high IQ or a large inheritance. Those factors may help, but they are not essential. According to Stanley, among the millionaires, "were mediocre students, but personable people."[1]

Your people skills—the way you interact with others—are the key to success at every level.

A New Attitude

What we have been discussing is more than how you deal with your associates. It concerns your attitude toward life itself.

How will you respond when there's a roadblock ahead? Where will you turn in a moment of crisis?

What will you say when the news is bleak?

It was a horrible snowstorm in North Carolina. Twelve inches fell in my hometown of Charlotte and up to two feet fell in the eastern part of the state. At about seven o'clock in the evening I was driving down the interstate on the way to the Charlotte Hornets NBA game with the Boston Celtics. Suddenly my new car hit an icy patch and began spinning out of control. We slammed into a guard rail, then bounced another fifty feet down into a ravine. My friend and I unbuckled our seat belts and surveyed the damage—several thousand dollars' worth. While I was on the mobile phone calling for a tow truck, four huge Hispanic men stopped and said, "Let us help you." They literally lifted my car out of the ditch back onto the highway. One of them said, as he pulled the twisted metal away from the front tire, "I think you can drive this thing."

"What are we going to do?" asked my friend. "We're going to the game!" I replied without hesitation. "It's only metal!" And we arrived at halftime. The Hornets beat the Celtics 110–96.

We called our wives from the coliseum and said, "Have we got a story to tell you!" Later, when we related the saga, my wife asked, "Why didn't you come straight home?"

"And miss a great game?" I replied.

Out of the Rut

Following a seminar on love-based leadership, a man in his fifties took me aside and said, "I like what you are telling me, but I'm too old to try a new management style. I served in the Marines, and the military mode of supervision is in my blood."

"Are you married?" I asked.

"Yes, we just celebrated our twenty-fifth anniversary," he proudly told me.

"Well, did your wife decide to marry you because you were demanding and controlling?"

"No," he countered. "With her it's totally different. She tells me I am the most loving guy in the world."

"I think it's time for a change," I encouraged him. "You need that same reputation at the office."

There's a great danger of staying in a rut. In France research has been conducted on what are called "processionary" caterpillars. These little creatures travel in long lines, simply following their leader. They march forward at the same pace, without considering their final destination. In one experiment a group of caterpillars was placed on the rim of a large flowerpot—with the leader of the group nose-to-tail with the last one in procession. It was a perfect circle and they kept going around and around.

In the middle of the flowerpot was a great cache of food. Yet the caterpillars kept circling, day after day, night after night. After seven days, one by one, they began dying of starvation.

Before it is too late, make a decision to alter your pattern.

Barry's Gift

How enduring is love? Let me tell you about Barry, an eight-year-old who wanted to give his mother a special Christmas present. He bought a plain white china plate and decided he would use his hobby paints at home to create something just for her.

That night, in his room, he painted green leaves and little red berries around the edges of the plate, and in the center he carefully added the words: "Merry Christmas, Mother."

When the paint dried he wrapped the plate in red paper, tied it with a gold ribbon, and placed it under the tree, counting the days until Christmas.

On December 25, Barry took the gift from under the tree and proudly handed it to his mother. She unwrapped the paper and there was his hand-painted Christmas plate—broken in three pieces.

Barry began to cry. "Oh, Mother," he said, "I painted it all by myself." He was heartbroken. His mother put her arms around him and said, "Don't worry, I'll fix it. We'll get it back together."

Years later, Barry's mother still treasures that mended plate. It is one of her prized possessions. You see, it is not the gift but the heart it represents that contains the meaning.

"I'd Make More Mistakes"

The next time you are overwhelmed by stress and tempted to lash out at those around you, think about these words by an unknown author:

If I had my life to live over, I'd dare to make more mistakes next time. I'd relax, I'd limber up. I would be sillier then I've been this trip. I would take fewer things seriously, take more chances, take more trips. I'd climb more mountains, and swim more rivers. I would, perhaps, have more actual troubles, but I'd have fewer imaginary ones. You see, I'm one of those people who lived seriously, sanely, hour after hour, day after day. Oh, I've had my moments, and if I had it to do over again, I'd have more of them. I've been one of those persons who never goes anywhere without a thermometer, a hot-water bottle, a raincoat, and a parachute. If I had to do it again, I would travel lighter than this trip. If I had my life to live over, I would start going barefoot earlier in the spring, and stay that way later in the fall. I would ride more merry-go-rounds. I would pick more daisies.

The good news is that there's still time!

REMINDERS FOR LEADERS WHO LOVE

- Build a partnership, not a kingdom.
- Love people, not programs.
- Involve others in your vision.
- Embrace mission-driven leadership.
- You are shaped by the principles you cherish.
- Kindness must become a lifestyle.
- Discover the dreams of others.
- See every associate as an equal.
- Allow people to discover answers for themselves.
- We win through cooperation, not competition.
- Have an open mind, not an agenda.
- Build alliances based on principles.
- Fulfillment comes through people, not things.

When the years pass and people reflect, what do they remember most? Is it the way they outsmarted a rival or gained leverage during a negotiation? No. They think about moments of great inspiration, the acts of kindness received from others, and the affection of their associates. Why? Because *love endures all things*.

There is a time to hold the gavel and a time to pass it on. More important than plaques on your wall or monuments bearing your name are the hearts that have been touched because you chose to lead with love.

Notes

Chapter 1

1. Al Capone, quoted in Louis E. Boone, *Quotable Business* (New York: Random House, 1992), 75.

2. Carlos Maria Giulini, quoted in Warren Bennis and Burt Nanus, *Leaders: The Strategy for Taking Charge* (New York: Harper & Row, 1985), 225.

3. William T. Solomon, quoted in L. J. McFarland, *21st Century Leadership* (Los Angeles: The Leadership Press, 1993), 186.

4. Tracy Goss, *The Last Word on Power* (New York: Doubleday, 1996), 11.

Chapter 2

1. John F. Welch Jr., quoted in Donald W. Blohowiak, *Mavericks!* (Homewood, Ill.: Business One, Irwin, 1992), 16.

2. Lester Bittel, *Leadership: The Key to Management Success* (New York: Franklin Watts, 1984), 8.

3. John P. Kotter, *A Force for Change* (New York: The Free Press, 1990), 63.

4. John R. Katzenbach, *Real Change Leaders* (New York: Times Books, 1995), 9.

5. David Pincus and J. Nicholas DeBois, *Top Dog* (New York: McGraw-Hill, 1994), 20.

6. Mary Kay Ash, quoted in Louis E. Boone, *Quotable Business* (New York: Random House, 1992), 42.

Chapter 3

1. Dwight D. Eisenhower, quoted in Louis E. Boone, *Quotable Business* (New York: Random House, 1992), 42.

2. Samuel Shultz, interview by author. October 1995.

Chapter 4

1. Ken Lipke, interview by author. 1991.

2. Leighton Ford, *Transforming Leadership* (Downers Grove, Ill.: InterVarsity Press, 1991), 99.

3. Ed Oakley and Doug Krug, *Enlightened Leadership* (New York: Simon & Schuster, 1991), 175.

4. Barbara Sher, *I Could Do Anything if I Only Knew What It Was,* online at *www.barnesandnoble.com.* 3 March 2000.

5. John P. Kotter, *A Force for Change* (New York: The Free Press, 1990), 36.

6. Warren Bennis and Burt Nanus, *Leaders: The Strategy for Taking Charge* (New York: Harper & Row, 1985), 109.

Chapter 5

1. Martin Luther King, quoted in William Safire, *Lend Me Your Ears: Great Speeches in History* (New York: W. W. Norton, 1992), 499.

2. Charles Winters, interview by author. November 1997.

3. Kenneth Wessner, quoted in Glenn Van Ekeren, *Speaker's Sourcebook II* (Englewood Cliffs, N.J.: Prentice-Hall, 1994), 256.

4. Ken Blanchard and Michael O'Connor, *Managing by Values* (San Francisco: Berrett-Koehler Publishers, 1997), 144.

5. Tom Chappell, *The Soul of a Business* (New York: Bantam Books, 1993), 183.

6. Southwest Airlines, quoted in Jeffrey Abrahams, *The Mission Statement Book* (Berkeley, Calif.: Ten Speed Press, 1995), 511.

7. Ibid., 61.

8. St Joseph's Hospital, Hamilton, Ontario, online at *www.stjosham.on.ca.* June 1998.

9. John R. Corts, quoted on the Billy Graham Evangelistic Association Internet site, online at *www.graham-assn.org.* January 1998.

10. Pat Ford Davis, quoted online at *www.crye-leike.com/patforddavis.* July 1998.

Chapter 6

1. Warren Bennis and Burt Nanus, *Leaders: The Strategy for Taking Charge* (New York: Harper & Row, 1985), 222.

2. James Dobson, quoted in Edythe Draper, *Quotations for the Christian World* (Wheaton Ill.: Tyndale House Publishers, 1992), 555.

Chapter 7

1. Sparky Anderson, quoted in Louis E. Boone, *Quotable Business* (New York: Random House, 1992), 20.

2. Galileo, quoted in Ed Oakley and Doug Krug, *Enlightened Leadership* (New York: Simon & Schuster, 1991), 166.

Chapter 8

1. Danny Cox, *Leadership When the Heat's On* (New York: McGraw-Hill, 1992), 37.

2. James Kouzes, *The Leadership Challenge* (San Francisco: Jossey-Bass Publishers, 1991), xiv.

3. David Allison, quoted in "Exercise Motivation," *Charlotte (N.C.) Observer,* 19 April 1999, A4.

4. Don Nelson, quoted in "Energizing Employees," *Charlotte (N.C.) Observer,* 25 February 1999, D2.

5. J. W. Marriott Jr., *The Spirit to Serve* (New York: HarperBusiness, 1997), 37.

6. Karl Menninger, quoted in *The Fairview Guide to Positive Quotations* (Minneapolis: Fairview Press, 1996), 173.

Chapter 9

1. Max DePree, *Leadership Is an Art* (New York: Dell Publishing, 1989), 10.

2. Charles M. Farkas and Philippe De Backer, *Maximum Leadership* (New York: Henry Holt & Company, 1996), 96.

3. Ibid., 3.

Chapter 10

1. Stuart Levine and Michael Crom, *The Leader in You* (New York: Simon & Schuster, 1993), 104.

2. Charles Handy, *The Hungry Spirit* (New York: Broadway Books, 1998), 125.

Chapter 11

1. Charles Dygert, *Success Is a Team Effort* (Columbus, Ohio: Motivational Enterprises Inc., 1993), 10.

2. Marcus Aurelius, quoted in Winston K. Pendleton, *Handbook of Inspirational Stories, Anecdotes and Humor* (West Nyack, N.Y.: Parker Publishing Company, 1982), 66.

3. Tom Chappell, *The Soul of a Business* (New York: Bantam Books, 1993), 69.

4. Terry L. Paulson, *They Shoot Managers, Don't They?* (Berkeley, Calif.: Ten Speed Press, 1991), 64.

Chapter 12

1. "Rudeness at Work on the Rise," Associated Press, 10 August 1999, online at *www.newsday.com/ap/topnews/index/htm.*

2. Lee Bowman, "Emotional Flu," *Nashville Tennessean,* 3 March 1999, D1.

3. Kenneth Cloke and Joan Goldsmith, *Thank God It's Monday!* (New York: Times Mirror, 1997), 155.

4. Peter Frost and Sandra Robinson, "The Toxic Handler," *Harvard Business Review,* July/August 1999, 34.

5. "Beethoven Soothes Nerves on Tense Korean Frontier," Reuters News, 27 April 1999, online at *www.dailynews.yahoo/com/headlines.*

Chapter 13

1. Brian Tracy, *Maximum Achievement* (New York: Fireside/Simon & Schuster, 1993), 259.

2. Edward Hallowell, quoted on *NBC Today,* 9 September 1999, online at *www.msnbc.com/news.*

3. "Staying Connected," NBC News report. 9 September 1999, online at *www.msnbc.com/news.*

4. William and Kathleen Lundin, *The Healing Manager* (San Francisco: Berrett-Koehler Publishers, 1993), xii.

5. Tom Watson Jr., quoted in Terry Paulson, *They Shoot Managers, Don't They?* (Berkeley, Calif.: Ten Speed Press, 1991), 60.

6. Philip Crosby, *Leading: The Art of Becoming an Executive* (New York: McGraw-Hill, 1990), 4.

7. Reg Jones, quoted in Mark Potts and Peter Behr, *The Leading Edge* (New York: McGraw-Hill, 1987), 202.

8. Albert Schweitzer, quoted in Louis E. Boone, *Quotable Business* (New York: Random House, 1992), 38.

Chapter 14

1. Daniel Goleman, *Working with Emotional Intelligence.* Book review, online at *www.barnesandnoble.com.* 17 June 2000.

2. Denis Waitley, *The Seeds of Greatness* (New York: Simon & Schuster, 1983), 159.

3. Connie Podesta and Jean Gatz, *How to Be the Person Successful Companies Fight to Keep* (New York: Simon & Schuster, 1997), 109.

4. Nido Quebein, *Communicate Like a Pro* (New York: Berkeley Publishing, 1983), 219.

5. Donald G. Krause, *The Way of the Leader* (New York: Pedigree/Berkeley Publishing, 1997), 90.

6. Harvey MacKay, quoted in Louis E. Boone, *Quotable Business* (New York: Random House, 1992), 59.

7. E. J. Pollock, "The Selling of a Golden Speech," *Wall Street Journal,* 2 March 1999, B1.

8. Burt Nanus, *The Leader's Edge* (Chicago: Contemporary Books, 1989), 54.

Chapter 15

1. Lester Bittel, *Leadership: The Key to Management Success* (New York: Franklin Watts, 1984), 118.

2. Donald Guthrie, *New Testament Theology* (Downers Grove, Ill.: InterVarsity Press, 1981), 107.

Chapter 16

1. Thomas Stanley, *The Millionaire Mind,* online review at *www.amazon.com.* 12 July 2000.

Neil Eskelin is a popular conference and seminar speaker as well as an author. Among his best-selling books are *The 24-Hour Turn-Around, Yes Yes Living in a No No World,* and *What to Do When You Don't Know What to Do.* His books have sold over a million copies and he has spoken to over a million people. You can contact the author at his e-mail address: neil@neileskelin.com